Illustrated
Weather Eye

BRENDAN MCWILLIAMS
COMPILED BY ANNE MCWILLIAMS

This book was designed and produced for
Gill & Macmillan
by Teapot Press Ltd

Text copyright © 2012 Anne McWilliams
Design copyright © 2012 Teapot Press Ltd

Compiled by Anne McWilliams

Gill & Macmillan
Hume Avenue, Park West,
Dublin 12
with associated companies
throughout the world
www.gillmacmillanbooks.ie

ISBN: 978-0-7171-5364-0

Printed in EU

Illustrated
Weather Eye

Dedication

To
Christopher, Stephen and Laurie

Thank you

Acknowledgements

I would like to thank my son, Stephen, and daughter, Laurie, whose warm recollections of their father helped me greatly with the selection of articles contained in this volume. Sincere thanks also to my wonderful friends for the patience they exhibited during the times I was preoccupied or unavailable, and for the unfailing support and encouragement they gave me throughout this whole project.

I am very grateful to Peter Lynch, Professor of Meteorology at UCD, who looked over the text in order to identify any gremlins of a scientific nature that may have crept in during the editing process, and to Jonathan Williams, my agent, whose expert help and advice were invaluable. Finally, I would like to thank the people at Gill & Macmillan who were, one and all, a delight to work with.

Storm in Harvest, 1856 (oil on canvas), **John Linnell (1792–1882)**
© The Drambuie Collection, Edinburgh, Scotland/The Bridgeman Art Library

Contents

Prologue

My husband was an erudite gentleman; an avid reader from childhood, his breadth of knowledge was extensive. He was also charming, vivacious and mischievously funny; all of which attributes, in addition to his love of literature, history and science, surfaced in his *Weather Eye* column over the years. Here, I have tried to select articles that demonstrate these aspects of his character so that the reader may delight in him afresh.

Weather Eye was born on 9 August 1988 – a bright, new, healthy baby that survived its infancy in the late eighties and thrived through its childhood and adolescence in the nineties. During that time Brendan had frequently strayed from the subject of the weather, exploring many other topics associated with meteorology. He was passionate about articulating scientific information in a way that was accessible to his readers and used every method he could to achieve that goal.

But it was in 2005, the first full year of his retirement, that he had more time to give to his writing. At home in Ireland, relaxing with his family and friends and freed from the considerable responsibilities of his administrative duties as Director of Administration for Eumetsat in Germany, his style developed a confident maturity as, daily, he wove a rich tapestry of beautifully crafted pen-pictures into an already well-established format.

While living in Germany from 1998 to 2004, we travelled a great deal: to and fro across the continent to international conferences and meetings that Brendan was obliged to attend. We made full use of our free time on these trips by searching for anything we could find of scientific, historical, literary or artistic note, and in doing so had the privilege of visiting many of the national galleries, major art collections and museums in Europe.

We journeyed mostly by car and rarely booked ahead, which afforded us the opportunity of unplanned stops along the way. Perhaps a Roman archaeological dig here, an ancient Celtic site there, a vineyard, a cathedral, Millet's studio in Barbizon, Monet's Giverny gardens, Arles where Van Gogh lived for a while, and even the prehistoric caves in Lascaux. We walked the streets of Rouen looking for literary links to Gustave Flaubert. We visited glaciers in Switzerland; salt mines in Austria; stopped, sat and watched in amazement as mini 'dust devils' formed in a field somewhere south of Seville. And coming home for our annual holiday, we regularly made a detour to attend a Shakespeare play in Stratford-upon-Avon.

Uppermost in Brendan's mind was his *Weather Eye* column. He sometimes likened himself to a magpie; any information he could gather or anything he could spot that he thought would be of interest to his readers was carefully logged and often found in *The Irish Times* within a few days. His annual pilgrimage to the Panthéon to see Foucault's Pendulum, which he wrote about on 28 September, was one such event, as were his observations and thoughts whilst peering at the street below from our hotel window on the Rive Gauche the previous day. We should not have been, but we always were, surprised when speaking to our friends in Ireland that they knew so much about our movements. On the bright side, we never had to worry too much about sending postcards.

I had great difficulty selecting the articles for this book; almost all were worthy of inclusion and difficult to leave out. There were several little gems, however, which could not be excluded. 'The Painful Face of the Weather', for example, and 'The Cleverness of *Tig A' Doicheall*', where Brendan nostalgically drew on recollections from his childhood in Waterville, County Kerry. His dry, tongue-in-cheek humour is exhibited in the first lines of 'Making the Best of April Showers' and 'Midsummer Measures'; his brilliant ability to inform is apparent in the clear and concise explanation of 'light scattering' in 'The Hues and Whys of Seas and Lakes'; and the delightful little discussions on bees in 'An Angry Summer in the Bee-Loud Glade' and 'The Dance of the Honey Bee' were a must.

In summary, I have chosen for this anthology articles that let Brendan speak once more: those that show his personality a little and those which, judging from his postbag at the time, seemed to capture the readers' imaginations. Starting in winter 2004, they are illustrated with pertinent images and some of the works of art that I know he enjoyed. I think he would have approved, and I hope you will enjoy them too.

Anne McWilliams
Greystones, Co. Wicklow
February 2012

The Statistics of Pseudo-White Eventualities

23 December 2004

Pity the poor weather-person at this time of year! At every social encounter, sooner or later he or she is asked: 'Are we going to have a White Christmas?' Not that everyone, I suppose, has ambitions to emulate the energetic Bob Cratchit who 'went down a slide on Cornhill twenty times, in honour of its being Christmas-eve'. But there does seem to be a lurking yen in many of us to see the festive season celebrated in the traditional Dickensian conditions.

Of course it all depends on what you mean by a white Christmas. Very often a single snowflake falling at a particular place within the 24 hours of Christmas Day may be enough to win a wager on the subject, Dublin Airport often being that designated spot. When you consider that snow in some shape or form is experienced at Dublin Airport on about three days in the average December, it suggests appropriate odds for this pseudo-white eventuality of about 10/1, or maybe somewhat less since the likelihood of snow increases as the month progresses. White Christmases, too, are more common in Ulster than down south, and the chances increase significantly with height above sea level.

But all in all, there have been only 12 Christmases since 1960 when snow fell over Ireland in any appreciable quantities, and on only five of these – 1962, 1964, 1970, 1980 and 1984 – could the snow have been described as widespread. The nearest we have come to a real white Christmas was over 40 years ago in 1962, when snow started on Christmas Day and continued on and off in many parts until New Year's Eve.

Bearing in mind this relative rarity of white Christmases, is it not strange that the cards we send each other at this time of year frequently show landscapes covered with several feet of snow? Skaters disport themselves on frozen ponds, buglers bugle from snow-entrenched mail-coaches, and little robins search for crumbs in the very cruellest blizzards.

The perennial white Christmas, however, is not entirely a figment of artistic licence. Most of our ideas about Yuletide are based on traditions from the eighteenth and nineteenth centuries, and in those times the white Christmas was a harsh reality. Europe was in the grip of the Little Ice Age, average temperatures were a degree or more lower than they are now, and snow at Christmastime was relatively common.

Of the first nine Christmases of Charles Dickens's life, for example, between 1812 and 1820, no fewer than six were white. Moreover, prior to the adoption of the reformed Gregorian Calendar in 1752, the 25th of December would have fallen in the part of the astronomical year that we now identify with early January – a time when snow is much more common than in late December. When Dickens was a lad, therefore, many older people still alive would have been able to tell him about the colder, harsher Christmases that prevailed when they, in turn, were young.

Scene on Ice (detail), c.1620 (oil on wood panel), **Hendrick Avercamp (1585–1634)**, National Gallery of Ireland

A Blizzard with a Happy Ending

27 December 2004

Travelling by car from Wexford to Dublin last Thursday evening, I was royally entertained by an episode of a dramatised version on RTÉ Radio 1 of R. D. Blackmore's romantic novel *Lorna Doone.* It brought back haunting memories of the adventures of Uncle Reuben, the Ridds and the highwayman Tom Faggus, and the fearsome family of Doones – the Counsellor, Sir Ensor and that most villainous of reprobates himself, the Carver Doone.

The Doones were an unruly, boisterous branch of the Scottish Stuart Clan, related to the Earls of Moray, who, having tested the patience of their relatives in Scotland, were banished in 1618 and had to take refuge down in England. They settled finally on Exmoor, where Sir Ensor Doone and his several sons brought terror to the local countryfolk, extorting by threats and outrage, raids and robberies, whatever they desired.

Blackmore's book contains one of the most vivid snowstorms to be found in English literature. It occurred during a very severe winter, which John Ridd describes most vividly: 'For a frost was beginning which made a great difference to Lorna and to myself – such a frost as I never saw before and neither hope to see again; it was a time when it was impossible to milk a cow for icicles, or for a man to shave some of his beard without blunting his razor on a hard grey ice.'

Now, we are given sufficient information in the book to deduce that Ridd is speaking of the 1680s. Moreover, meteorological records tell us that the winter of 1683/84 was the severest ever known in southern Britain, when the 'Little Ice Age' was at its very height. It is reasonable, therefore, to assign to this particular winter the ferocious but very helpful blizzard which allows John Ridd to rescue his beloved Lorna from Glen Doone. In one of the most evocative weather passages in the English language, Blackmore describes the snow as 'rolling and curling beneath the violent blast, tufting and combing with rustling swirls, and carved like a cornice where the grooving chisel of the wind has swept round; ever and again the tempest snatches little whiffs from the channelled edges, twirls them round and makes them dance over the chine of the monster pile, then lets them lie like herring-bones or the seams of sand where once the tide has been.'

Unpleasant as this may seem to you and me, the snow was singularly helpful to John Ridd and Lorna: 'To my great delight, I found that the weather, not often friendly to lovers, and lately seeming so hostile, had in the most important matter done me a signal service.' And all ends well. It fittingly turns out that Lorna Doone is not a Doone at all, but a member of a good and noble family who had been kidnapped by the villains as a child. John and Lorna marry, and everyone – except, of course, the nasty Doones – lives happily ever after.

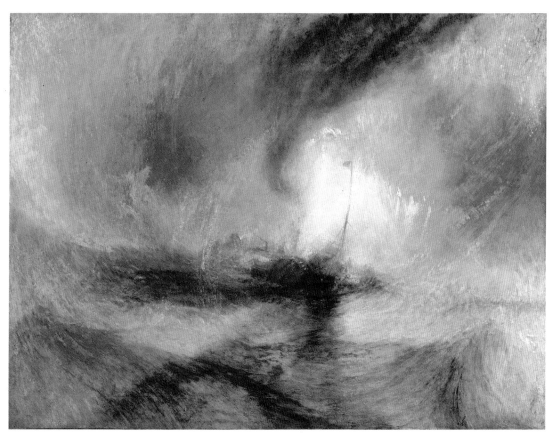

Snow Storm – Steam Boat off a Harbour's Mouth, 1842 (oil on canvas),
Joseph Mallord William Turner (1775–1851), Tate Collection

Fizzy-Drink Meteorology

5 January 2005

In meteorology, the term 'freezing fog' describes a situation where visibility is reduced by water droplets suspended in the air at a time when the temperature is zero or below. It often results in the formation of *rime*, a white, feathery, crystalline, opaque deposit which occurs when the water droplets, blown along by the breeze, hit a vertical surface and are transformed immediately to ice. It can be seen building up on the windward side of obstacles like clotheslines, garden railings, shrubs or overhead electrical power lines.

But surely the very existence of freezing fog is paradoxical? If the temperature falls below zero, should not those little drops of water in the air be transformed immediately into little lumps of ice?

The key to freezing fog lies in the fact that, contrary to what most of us might think, ice does not always form at 0°C. The freezing point of water, in fact, is not fixed at all, but varies widely depending on the circumstances; it merely has a maximum value of 0°C. To put it another way, water will never freeze when the temperature is above zero, but it may well remain liquid far into the zone of negative temperatures. This 'supercooled' state, however, is very unstable, and supercooled water will freeze very quickly given the right conditions – given a scaffolding of some sort on which the ice can form.

With a bottle of fizzy drink and a modicum of patience, you can watch the rapid freezing of supercooled water in the comfort of your kitchen. All you have to do is pop a bottle of your favourite fizzy tipple into the freezer, leave it for the right amount of time, and then gently take it out and stand it on the table top. Slowly remove the cap, and you will see the liquid almost instantaneously turn to ice in front of your very eyes.

Inside the freezer, you see, the drink becomes very cold indeed, cold enough to freeze in fact, except for the fact that ice crystals need something to hold on to, and inside the unopened drink there is little or nothing that can serve this purpose. But with the bottle-top removed, little fountains of bubbles suddenly appear. Ice crystals, as it happens, have no trouble holding on to bubbles, or on to crystals previously formed; so from the time the first ice crystal forms on the first bubble, it takes hardly any time at all for millions of crystals to form by chain reaction – hence the instantaneous freeze.

The tricky part of the above experiment is finding out for how long to leave the bottle in the freezer. If the interval is too short, the water will not be 'supercooled' enough; if it is too long, the fizzy drink will freeze *in situ*, probably bursting its bottle in the process. The answer must be sought, as men of science say, empirically – by finding out the hard way.

Mallard and Rime Frost, 1994 (oil on canvas), **Julian Novorol (born 1949)**
Private Collection/The Bridgeman Art Library

The Sounds of the Storm

10 January 2005

We have known what it is like, these past few days,

> *To be imprisoned in the viewless winds,*
> *And blown with restless violence round about*
> *The pendant world.*

Even those of us lucky enough to have escaped the physical effects of this onslaught have had to endure, at the very least, the unsettling and seemingly interminable howling of the gales, as the wind has swirled around the corners of buildings, swept over their chimneys and descended in violent cataracts from their gable ends. The sounds are produced by the endless succession of eddies produced in the wind by the obstacles in its path; sometimes these eddies, these 'flutterings' of the air, are of an appropriate frequency to be audible to the human ear.

Some of the notes, too, occur when the wind passes over cavities in rocks or buildings, and sets up forced vibrations in the air within them. The pitch of a note produced in this way depends on the dimensions of the cavity; a light breeze over a sea-shell produces a relatively high-pitched sound, while a low-pitched howl results when the wind strikes the opening of a large cavern. Most of us have also experienced in recent days,

> *. . . the dismal rain*
> *Comes down in slanting lines,*
> *And Wind, that grand old harper, smote*
> *His thunder-harp of pines.*

This 'thunder-harp', as the poet loosely calls it, has clearly nothing to do with thunder, but can be heard when the wind interacts with trees, passing around a myriad twigs and branches to produce notes that vary widely in their pitch and volume. The resulting medley can range from the friendly rustle of the leaves on a summer's day to the often plaintive murmur of a great oak in a gale; from the sibilant

The Winds Blowing Across the Lake at Lough Bray, Selina Crampton (1777–1858),
Private Collection, London

sigh of a single conifer to the mournful dirge of a forest of the larger pines in gale-
force winds.

These sounds are of similar origin to those that emanate from a length of wire
stretched before the wind. Such a wire disturbs the flow of air, causing it to break
up into a sequence of little eddies that are carried on downstream, and which may
sometimes be of a frequency to be heard as a musical note. The frequency of the
eddies increases with the speed of the wind, thus increasing the pitch of the audible
note, and decreases the greater the diameter of the wire or twig.

The overall effect is powerfully described by Sebastian Junger in his novel *The
Perfect Storm*: 'Fishermen say they can gauge how fast the wind is blowing by the
sound it makes against the wire stays and outrigger cables. A scream means the wind
is around Force 9 on the Beaufort Scale, 40 or 50 knots. Force 10 is a shriek. Force 11
is a moan, and over Force 11 is something the fishermen don't want to hear.'

Gale Warnings Down the Years

18 January 2005

The first gale warnings in a form vaguely recognisable to us now began to appear early in the second half of the nineteenth century. The man responsible in these parts was Vice-Admiral Robert FitzRoy, Head of the Meteorological Department of the British Navy. The potential for weather forecasting of the newly invented electric telegraph was quickly realised, and FitzRoy was charged with inaugurating a network of weather stations around the Irish and British coasts to undertake daily observations of the local weather. Reports from about 40 such stations were sent every day to the Admiralty in London, and used to try to anticipate the arrival of impending storms. When it seemed appropriate, a 'storm warning' ensued.

Strictly speaking, the storm warnings were not forecasts, since warnings were promulgated only when gales were already reported from one or more of the coastal stations. But they served their purpose as the shipping forecasts of their day. They were telegraphed to the relevant ports and harbours around Britain, and within 30 minutes appropriate signals were prominently displayed on shore to relay word of the expected storms to passing ships.

The signals were first employed in January 1864, and were of a semaphore type, comprising large wooden 'cones' or 'drums' hoisted to the top of a tall mast. If gales were expected from a generally northerly direction, a black cone, three feet high and three feet wide at the base, was raised; this was a 'North cone'. If, on the other hand, the gales were expected from a southerly quarter, a 'South cone' was hoisted – a cone with its apex pointing downwards.

A 'drum' or cylinder was sometimes used to indicate successive gales from varying directions, and at night red lights were used to indicate the shapes; a triangle of lights would form a cone, and four lights arranged in a square would indicate a drum. In all cases the signal was lowered when the wind dropped below gale force, provided no further gales were reckoned to be imminent; a signal still in evidence after the wind had dropped was to be interpreted as a sign that any abatement would be only temporary.

The use of semaphores gradually died out when radio became available. 'Wireless telegraphy' from ship to shore was first used for weather information as far back as 1907, and the first gale warnings for the waters around Ireland and Britain were relayed in Morse code to ships in the eastern North Atlantic in 1911. Then the first radio weather forecast in voice form was broadcast by the BBC on 14 November 1922; it applied only to London, but a general forecast for the whole of the UK began to be broadcast in 1924. A year later it was extended once daily to include an account of the general meteorological situation, a shipping forecast and, of course, any gale warnings in operation at the time.

The Gale on the Sea is Over, 1839 (oil on canvas), Ivan Aivazovsky (1817–1900)
© *The State Tretyakov Gallery, Moscow, Russia*

Shaken to a Shorter Day

21 January 2005

Have you noticed the days a little shorter since St. Stephen's Day? Well, maybe not, since the shortening has been a mere 2.68 microseconds in the 24 hours. Nonetheless, the tragic events in the Indian Ocean that day – not the tsunami itself, but rather the underwater earthquake in which it had its origins – had the side-effect of causing the Earth to rotate a little faster on its axis than it did before.

It all has to do with a principle known as the 'Conservation of Angular Momentum'. Momentum – roughly 'weight multiplied by speed' – represents something like a 'quantity of motion'; *angular momentum*, by extension, represents a 'quantity of rotation'. The latter depends on the rate of spin of an object, and on the distance of the various parts of the object from its axis of rotation. It is a cardinal principle of physics, from the atom to the cosmos, that in the absence of any external influences, angular momentum is 'conserved'; it always remains constant.

It follows from this that in the case of a rotating system, if there is a shift of weight away from the axis of rotation – thereby increasing the 'distance' part of the equation, there will be a compensating reduction in the rate of spin, and *vice versa*, so that the product of the two quantities will always stay unchanged. The principle can be seen at work in the case of a swimmer somersaulting from a high diving board; she can increase her rate of spin by doubling up her body. Likewise, a ballet dancer doing a pirouette with arms outstretched can spin more rapidly by drawing in his limbs, thereby decreasing the distance of several parts of his anatomy from his axis of rotation.

Now, as a first approximation, the Earth-atmosphere system can be regarded as free from external influence, and therefore its angular momentum must remain unchanged. Moreover, when the earthquake occurred under the Indian Ocean and the India tectonic plate slid down beneath the overriding Burma plate, the net effect was a slightly more 'compact' planet. The Earth's *oblateness* – the name given to the flattening at the poles and the bulging at the equator – decreased by a very small amount, about one part in 10 billion. And in order for angular momentum to be conserved, this net movement of mass towards the centre had to be compensated for by an increase in the Earth's speed of rotation – hence the shorter day.

This change in day-length is much too small to be observed; it can only be calculated. More measurable in due course, however, will be another consequence of the shifting masses on the Earth's crust on 26 December last year – a movement of about 2.5 cm, or one inch, in the position of the North Pole.

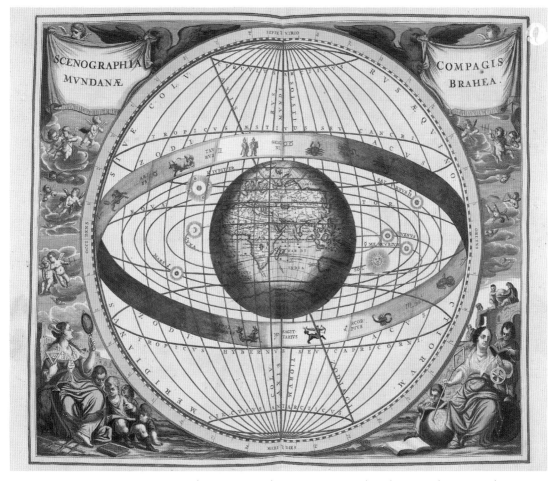

Harmonia Macrocosmica, Amsterdam, 1660. Plate representing the planets' orbits according to the Tychonic system, **Tycho Brahe (1546–1601)**. *Milan, Biblioteca Ambrosiana. © 2012.* © Veneranda Biblioteca Ambrosiana/De Agostini Picture Library/Scala, Florence

A Military Victory on Ice

24 January 2005

The French in the 1790s were anything but popular. European royalty were upset at the treatment meted out to their Bourbon cousins, and had an uneasy feeling that this Revolutionary rot might spread were they not to nip it in the bud. The French, for their part, wanted to pursue their own peculiar brand of *Liberté, Egalité, Fraternité, sans* interference from the outside world, and regarded the other Continental powers and Britain as a threat. Thus it was that in due course the new Republic found itself at war with nearly everyone, while nervous monarchs around Europe quickly forged alliances against it, and broke them just as easily as each one petulantly quarrelled with the others.

The climate of northern Europe mirrored this unrest. The continent was beginning to emerge from the cold period that has been dubbed the Little Ice Age, but the generally mild and pleasant 1790s produced one very severe winter, that of 1794–95. The prevailing temperate westerlies were absent for a time from northern Europe, and high pressure over Sweden and Finland allowed great pools of very cold air to drain from the interior of Russia and Siberia down over Denmark, northern Germany and the Netherlands. This, in turn, made possible a very strange victory indeed, unique in military annals: it allowed a small group of French cavalry to capture an entire Dutch fleet.

After a period of near civil war in Holland, Prince William V had fled to Britain on 18 January 1795, just as French troops began to advance into the Netherlands. Meanwhile, 15 Dutch ships were anchored off the island of Texel, adjacent to the town of Den Helder on the North Sea coast. It being the winter that it was, the coastal waters had frozen solid, and so the fleet was ice-bound.

Thus it was that on the morning of 24 January, 210 years ago today, a small troop of cavalry was able to ride across the ice and address the captain of the Dutch flagship, the *Admiraal Piet Heyn*. The cavalry commander, afterwards Lieutenant-General Lahure but at that time a young subaltern, recalled the bizarre event in later years: 'Before dawn I had taken position in the dunes. When the ships saw us, they prepared their defences. I sent some tirailleurs ahead, and followed with the rest of my forces.'

Opinions differ as to the extent to which the Dutch intended to resist, and as to whether French assault, such as it was, was based on persuasion, threat, or some *ad hoc* but understandable Dutch conversion to the cause of the Republic; in any event the *Admiraal Piet Heyn* surrendered, and was followed shortly afterwards, one by one, by all the other well-armed men o' war. 'The fleet was taken,' Lieutenant-General Lahure goes on, 'and the sailors received us *de bonne grâce* on board'.

The cavalry, one might say, had won a naval battle.

The French cavalry takes the Dutch fleet trapped in the ice at the port of Den Helder in the waters off Texel, 21 January 1795, **Charles Mozin** (1806–62)
© RMN / Château de Versailles

The Birthday of a Snowflake Man

9 February 2005

Wilson Alwyn Bentley dedicated his entire adult life to photographing snowflakes. He was born 140 years ago today on 9 February 1865, near Jericho, Vermont, and when he was 20 years of age, using a microscope and a camera in combination during a snowstorm, he took the first ever photographic image of an ice crystal.

There are billions and billions of snowflakes in every shower of snow. Each is an aggregate of many hundreds of tiny hexagonal ice crystals, even the largest of which are only a millimetre or two in diameter. Bentley had to work very rapidly to capture his photographs before the ice crystals changed their shape by melting, and he learned how to enhance his images with transmitted light by pointing his camera towards the sky. Nowadays there are techniques to make such photography much easier; collected snowflakes can be plunged into a cup of liquid nitrogen at more than 100 degrees below zero Celsius, and at this very low temperature the crystals can be coated with platinum, allowing them to retain their shape indefinitely. But no such high-tech methods were available to Bentley; he had only his dedication, his innate patience, and his skill.

He was a quiet, gentle, unassuming man, but he approached his snowflakes with the incisive eye of both the poet and the scientist. 'A careful study of the internal structure', he wrote, 'not only reveals a new and far greater elegance of form than that exhibited by the simple outlines, but by means of these wonderfully delicate and exquisite figures, much may be learned of the history of each crystal, and the changes through which it has passed in its journey through the cloudland. Was ever a life history written in more dainty hieroglyphics!'

Bentley kept detailed meteorological records, and pondered over the shapes and sizes of his crystals, wondering why they often varied from one shower to the next. His photographs convinced him that different segments of a storm produced their own predominant type of ice crystal, and that the texture of an individual crystal was related to the different temperatures it had experienced. He went on to suggest that the atmospheric circulation within a storm could be deduced from the various crystalline structures of the snowflakes, a theory that was decades ahead of the meteorological thinking of his time.

By 1920, Wilson Bentley had a worldwide reputation as 'the Snowflake Man', and his 'photomicrographs' were eagerly sought after by jewellers, engravers and by designers in the textile industry. By 1931, he had built up a collection of more than 6,000 images, each of an individual snow crystal entirely different from any of the others. He died that year, just days before his book, *Snow Crystals*, featuring over 2,000 of his pictures and destined to become a meteorological classic in the years that followed, appeared upon the bookshelves.

Examples of photographs by **Wilson Bentley**

Digital Archives of the Jericho Historical Society
Wilson Bentley, snowflakebentley.com

The Painful Face of the Weather

15 February 2005

Does anybody suffer nowadays from corns? When I was a lad, many mega-moons ago, all the oldies in my local village were forever complaining of their corns, and would exchange lengthy homilies on how to deal with them. But corns, if they exist at all today, seem to be suffered in a universal conspiracy of total silence.

This, in some ways, is a pity, because it was well known in those days that active corns were an infallible precursor of the rain. Hence the well-known rhyme:

Old Betty's joints are on the rack;
Her corns and shooting pains torment her,
And to her bed untimely send her.

There is no direct scientific evidence, that I know of, to support the corn thesis. It is true, however, that scar tissue, corns and other abnormal skin have rates of expansion and contraction different from normal skin, so a sudden rise in the humidity prior to the onset of rain might cause nerve endings to trigger sufficient pain to send Betty, untimely, to her bed.

But what of poor Betty's other ailments? Now, this is a subject on which there has been some research. It was noted in experiments carried out a century and a half ago, for example, that wounded soldiers seemed to suffer more pain in conditions of falling atmospheric pressure and rising temperature and humidity than they did at other times. But the studies most often quoted in this context are those carried out by a Dr. Joseph Hollander of Pennsylvania.

Hollander used a 'Controlled Climate Chamber', constructed so that it could comfortably house two patients for about four weeks. The patients chosen for observation were carefully selected as 'weather-sensitive', sufferers from arthritis or rheumatism who claimed that changes in the weather worsened or improved their symptoms.

Temperature, pressure and humidity within the chamber could be carefully controlled. For part of the duration, 'atmospheric' conditions were kept constant; at

Sleepy Old Woman, 1656 (oil on canvas),
Nicolaes Maes (1634–93), Royal
Museums of Fine Arts of Belgium, Brussels

other times pressure alone was varied by perhaps 20 hectopascals in a 24-hour period; at other times humidity alone was allowed to change; and sometimes both were changed together, mimicking the conditions typical of an approaching warm front. Meanwhile, each patient noted the severity and duration of any pains, and regular objective checks were carried out on the tenderness or swelling of susceptible joints.

By and large, variations of pressure alone, or humidity alone, induced no symptoms, but when there was a simultaneous fall in pressure and a rise in the humidity, patients experienced an increase in pain, a discomfort that was alleviated when conditions settled down again. Moreover, a succession of such changes, corresponding to what might be called a 'stormy' interlude in real life, appeared to have a cumulative effect.

The conclusion was that Old Betty's joints are a reliable indicator of the weather after all. But why this should be so in such a complex way, no one really knows.

Any Fungus in a Famine

28 February 2005

You may have noticed from time to time that old gravestones are frequently disfigured by large growths of irregular shape in many different pastel shades; they often cover the lettering on the stonework, making it very difficult to read. But if they are aesthetically questionable, these lichens, as they are called, are in themselves a welcome sign. Although they can endure the most extreme climatic conditions, they are very sensitive to any impurities in the air, and a thriving population of lichens is an indication that the local air is clean.

Lichens are a strange and unique form of life comprising a symbiotic pairing of a fungus and an alga. They form most readily on the barks of trees, on rocks and, as we have seen, on gravestones. Individuals may grow by as little as a millimetre a year, but they can survive for centuries, and even, for all we know, millennia.

Some parts of the world have exotic varieties of these strange organisms, and the locals have been inventive in their use of them. *Leconora esculenta*, for example, is a rather flaky lichen which peels easily from the rocks in the arid regions where it thrives, to blow freely in the wind. When a severe famine affected certain areas near the Caspian Sea in 1829, the countryside became littered with *Leconora esculenta* after a violent wind-storm. The local populace, noticing that their sheep could eat it without ill-effect, gathered the lichen, ground it down to flour, and made it into what was apparently a very palatable bread.

And, of course, we all know the biblical story about the manna falling down from heaven. It is related in the Book of Exodus how the Israelites, having survived their difficulties with Pharaoh at the Red Sea, found themselves in the wilderness of Sur with very little food. 'Murmurings' began to surface against Moses. 'Would to God,' his followers complained, 'we had died by the hand of the Lord in the land of Egypt, when we sat over the flesh pots, and ate bread to the full.'

Divine help, however, was at hand. The Lord said to Moses: 'Behold, I will rain bread from heaven for you: let the people go and gather what is sufficient for every day.' And so He did: 'In the morning a dew lay round about the camp,' and when the dew was gone, 'thin flakes like unto the hoar frost on the ground' appeared upon the desert floor. The Israelites duly gathered up the manna and made it into bread to eat.

Now scientists, while never ruling out the possibility of direct intervention from Above, have suggested that the biblical manna may well have been *Leconora esculenta,* and the Israelites had a fortuitous experience very similar to that which proved such a life-saver in the Caspian region in 1829.

The Miracle of the Manna, c.1577 (oil on canvas), Jacopo Tintoretto (1518–94)
Wikimedia Commons

A Rough and Rowdy Month

1 March 2005

For meteorologists, winter is over and spring sprang this morning. Some, of course, might think us somewhat hasty in bringing winter to a close so soon; astronomers, for instance, celebrate the birth of spring at the vernal equinox in two or three weeks' time. Others inhabit an *ancien régime*, a time-warp in which the season starts a month ago. But for us, March and spring are perennial twins, forever born again today.

March is an adolescent month, always unsure of itself and full of bluff and bluster. At times it has an atavistic streak, reverting to its wintry origins, but now and then its lengthening days show promise, and hint at better times to come. Because of its boisterous winds, the ancient Saxons called it 'rough month', *Hreth-monath*; to the revolutionary French it was *Ventose* – 'the windy one'; we, on the other hand, call it irrelevantly after Mars, the Roman god of war.

If March this year were to behave according to the norm, it would see Ireland for much of the time under the influence of a regular procession of vigorous depressions, each one following the other across the Atlantic at intervals of 36 hours or so. Their energy derives from the contrast in temperature between the equator and the poles, which is near maximum at this time of year. It was a typical March depression, for example, which sank the *HMS Eurydice* off Ventnor in March 1878, and caused Gerard Manley Hopkins to exclaim:

> *And you were a liar, O blue March day.*
>
> . . . .
>
> *A beetling baldbright cloud through England*
> *Riding: there did storms not mingle? and*
> *Hailropes hustle and grind their*
> *Heavengravel? wolfsnow, worlds of it, wind there?*

Those of you who have mastered *Finnegans Wake* in its entirety will immediately grasp precisely what he means.

*Printemps à
Giverny, 1903
(oil on canvas),*
Claude Monet
(1840–1926)
Private Collection/
Giraudon
The Bridgeman Art
Library

Yet despite its reputation as a windy month, the average wind speed in Ireland in March is significantly less than that in February, and there are fewer gales. The reason is probably related to the average paths of the Atlantic depressions, which with the onset of spring tend to follow a more northerly track, and so most of them have a less devastating effect on our island than their winter cousins.

The air temperature in March often rises to an average of 10° or 11°C each day. The highest March temperature ever recorded in Ireland was 24 degrees in Dublin in 1965, and the lowest was minus 17 degrees on 3 March in the memorably cold year of 1947. Usually there is a marked decrease this month, compared to February, in the occurrence of both ground and air frost.

Rainfall in March, normally between 50 and 100mm in low-lying areas, marks the transition between January and February – statistically the two wettest months of the Irish year – and the relatively dry period we normally enjoy from April through to June.

Gender and Seasonal Insanity

2 March 2005

'In general the senses of men are coarse and dull, and void of energy,' wrote Richard Inwards, the nineteenth-century guru on traditional weather lore. 'But animals,' he went on, 'which retain their natural instincts, which have their organs better constituted and their senses in a more perfect state, unchanged by vicious and depraved habits, perceive sooner, and are more susceptible to, the impressions produced in them by variations in the atmosphere, and sooner exhibit signs of them.'

Now, my wife, peering over my left shoulder at what nonsense I might be writing for today, light-heartedly pointed out to me that Mr Inwards's second sentence could more aptly be applied to women, not animals, thereby making his general thesis indisputable. But this is a distraction politely to ignore. The point is that, as written by Inwards, the theory explains why, some time before snow is due, hares forsake the hills and scurry down into the valleys. Of course, this alleged behaviour may not be factual at all, any more than that other leporine connection with the weather: the belief that the presence of a hare on board a ship guarantees a severe storm during the voyage.

The hare's most famous idiosyncrasy, however, is that remarked upon by Alice as she joined the Mad Hatter and his companion at that famous tea party. She surmised that 'the March Hare will be much more interesting, and perhaps as this is May, it won't be raving mad – at least not so mad as it was in March'. But why should hares be lunatics this month? Or as the issue is addressed in Walter Scott's *Rob Roy*: 'Wherefore a hare should be mad at March mair than at Martinmas, is mair than I can weel say.'

Hares are mainly solitary creatures, except during their breeding season which occurs around this time of year. And as in the case of humans, the amorous enthusiasm of competing males sometimes results in strange antics, including bounding to and fro, wild kicking, and the curious spectacle of protagonists standing on hind legs and appearing to box with one another. This unrestrained exuberance during the rutting season, compared to other times of year, has led to the expression 'mad as a March hare', and also lies behind the description of bizarre, foolhardy ideas or behaviour as being 'hare-brained'.

There is a story, too, about how hares acquired one of their best-known features. At the dawn of time, it seems, the Moon looked down and noticed that everyone was very much afraid of dying. She decided that the hare, known for its fleetness, would make a good messenger of hope: 'Tell them,' said the Moon, 'that everyone, like me, in dying will be renewed again.' But the giddy hare got the message totally mixed up, and the Moon was so angry that it bit the hare on the lip, where the mark remains to this day.

Hare, 1502 (watercolour on paper), **Albrecht Dürer (1471–1528)**, Graphische Sammlung Albertina, Vienna, Austria/The Bridgeman Art Library

The Cleverness of *Tig A' Doicheall*

4 March 2005

When I was very young and still at school, the road from Waterville to Cahirciveen was yet unmetalled. It was, by Kerry standards, not a winding road, and it had two long stretches cutting straight across the bog. On one of these, on the edge of Aghatubrid Bog, was *tig a' doicheall.*

The epithet was earned by the way the house was built. Rather than having a door that faced the road, which was the usual custom, the house presented a blank wall to the traveller passing by, the entrance being located round the 'back'. It was said that this had been done deliberately, to discourage farmers and jobbers driving their cattle to or from the fair at Cahirciveen from entering, to avail of the warmth and the shelter of the kitchen as a place to light their pipes. Hence it was *tig a' doicheall,* 'the house of no welcome'.

In retrospect, of course, it is clear that the design of the house had nothing whatsoever to do with hospitality, or lack of it. The builder, probably back in the nineteenth century, had very sensibly sited his door in such a way that it would be well protected from the prevailing, and usually very strong, southwesterly wind blowing straight across the bog from Ballinskelligs Bay.

Climatological foresight of this kind pays dividends in terms of the general amenity of any dwelling house. Of equal importance nowadays is the fact that large quantities of energy are lost from a building during cold conditions when the wind sweeps heat away from exposed surfaces; the panoramic view from a hilltop house may be impressive, but it is not enjoyed without significant cost. A location more sheltered by the local landscape, on the other hand, will be much more energy-efficient; stands of trees, too, can often be grown to act as effective natural wind-breaks, and indeed existing buildings can serve the same purpose if they happen to be there.

Houses can also be designed to take best advantage of available sunshine. In summer, too much sun is undesirable, and makes a house too hot; but in the wintertime, the sun is a valuable source of heat that should be tapped and husbanded.

The summer sun, being high in the sky, is easy to exclude by means of roof overhangs, awnings, or other overhead barriers; indeed, in our climate excessive heat is not a frequent problem. But capturing the winter sun requires more foresight.

The sun in winter rises in the southeast and sets in the southwest, so only windows facing due south, or close to it, let in much sunshine. The shrewd designer will bear this in mind, together with the fact that the benefits of a south-facing window can be enhanced by arranging that a substantial concrete wall lies directly opposite; it absorbs heat during the day for release at night, just like a giant storage heater.

Country Road (oil on board), **Markey Robinson** (1918–99), Private Collection
Photo © Bonhams, London, UK/Bridgeman Art Library

All Creatures Great and Small

12 March 2005

Carl Bergmann, a nineteenth-century German biologist, noticed a curious pattern to the average size attained by warm-blooded animals of the same species. His principle, known nowadays as 'Bergmann's Rule', states that the smaller sub-species of a particular species are to be found in the warmer parts of the ecological range, and that the larger races inhabit the cooler districts. The largest member of the cat family, for example, is the Siberian tiger, while the biggest of the bears, about eight feet tall when rearing up, is the polar bear, found only in the extreme northern latitudes inside the Arctic Circle.

Bergmann's Rule is assumed to be an evolutionary consequence of the mathematical fact that as a three-dimensional object increases in size, the ratio between its surface area and its volume diminishes. If, for example, you double the length, width and height of an object, its volume increases by a factor of eight while the surface area grows only by a factor of four. It follows that the bigger an animal happens to be, the smaller the area of skin it has in relation to its bulk. Since body heat is lost mainly through the skin, a large body therefore becomes an advantage in a cold environment where heat conservation is important.

But does it all stop there? Some observers of nature, mindful of Cecil Alexander's delightful little hymn which tells us that

> *All things bright and beautiful,*
> *All creatures great and small,*
> *All things wise and wonderful:*
> *The Lord God made them all,*

have asserted that He also applied this principle to human beings. They assert that a relationship exists between the weight of the average member of an ethnic group, and the latitude of the indigenous zone to which that group belongs.

In this part of the world, for example, we are told that an average Finn weighs 154lbs, a Spaniard 132lbs, and a typical Berber of Algeria 124lbs. Similarly in Asia, the average weight of the northern Chinese is alleged to be 142lbs, that of inhabitants of Laos and Vietnam 112lbs, and the Andaman Islanders of the Bay of Bengal 98lbs. The average indigenous inhabitant of the Kalahari Desert weighs in at a mere 89lbs. Some biologists have seen in this alleged phenomenon an application to the human species of the biological principle of 'Bergmann's Rule'; they infer from statistics such as these that average weight increases with distance from the equator – or more specifically, with the decrease in average annual temperature.

But as you might expect, it is more generally accepted that the application of Bergmann's Rule to the human race is highly suspect. Ethnic differences in weight can be more confidently explained, for example, by differences in the kind and quantity of foods available, or by differences in metabolic rates, than by any reference to the prevailing climate.

The Dream, 1912 (oil on canvas), **Franz Marc (1880–1916)**, *Madrid, Museo Thyssen-Bornemisza.* © 2012. Museo Thyssen-Bornemisza/Scala, Florence

A Little More About Cecil

14 March 2005

If you read *Weather Eye* on Saturday, you may recall that I quoted a few lines from Cecil Alexander's 'All Things Bright and Beautiful'. Of course you will know the hymn very well, even if, like me, you cannot hear it without thinking of James Herriot.

But I discovered an interesting fact or two about Cecil Alexander. Firstly, Cecil was a woman. She was born Cecil Frances Humphreys in Dublin in 1818, the daughter of Major John Humphreys, land-agent to the 4th Earl of Wicklow. In 1850, she married Rev. William Alexander of Termonamongan, near Strabane, their courtship being greatly facilitated, no doubt, by Cecil's extraordinary prolificacy in writing hymns. And they did very well; in 1867 William became Bishop of Derry and Raphoe, and Cecil joined him in the Episcopal Palace as – to coin a phrase – his Lady Bishopess.

But the other serendipitous nugget of information to pan out was that Cecil, still a Humphreys at that stage, wrote *All Things Bright and Beautiful* in 1848 while she was a guest of the Cooper family at Markree Castle, Collooney, Co. Sligo. Now, for weatherpeople, mention of the Coopers and Markree strikes not just a familiar chord, but sounds the overture to an entire meteorological concerto. Markree Castle is celebrated in the annals of both astronomy and Irish meteorology.

Science at Markree could be said to have begun with the birth of Edward Cooper in 1798. As a young man in the early 1820s Edward travelled extensively in the Middle East and Africa, and then, on his father's death in 1830, he took over the Markree estates. He installed a telescope at the Castle, and ultimately established an observatory whose reputation for many years almost equalled that at Birr. But more importantly for meteorologists, Edward Cooper established Markree Castle as a weather station, whose meteorological records were to be unrivalled in their duration anywhere in the west of Ireland, and rarely equalled in the country as a whole.

Weather observations had, in fact, begun in 1824, but the readings were sporadic. Under Edward Cooper's stewardship, however, a faultless series of daily readings was produced, lasting from 1833 until his death in 1863. His successor, his nephew Lt-Col. Edward Henry Cooper, had little interest in either astronomy or weather;

the observatory was largely dismantled, but the meteorology continued, even if the reports had once again become sporadic.

Edward Henry's reign at Markree lasted until 1874, and then, meteorologically speaking, things improved again. From 1875 onwards a complete, continuous record of the daily weather at Collooney is available, right up to the present day. It is the only series of weather observations from the west of Ireland that has lasted for longer than a century.

Markree Castle, Collooney, Co. Sligo, **Alexey Zarodov**
© 2012 photos.com

Products of a Meteoric Splash

30 March 2005

When Jupiter, the chief god of the ancient world, noticed something which displeased him going on below, he would intervene by hurling thunderbolts at all and sundry. As Shakespeare has him say in *Cymbeline,*

> *. . . How dare you ghosts*
> *Accuse the thunderer, whose bolt, you know,*
> *Sky-planted batters all rebelling coasts.*

There was a time when it was believed that the detritus of Jupiter's tantrums could be found in certain places here on Earth. Tektites, for example, are small glassy objects, pale green to black in colour, and are found in the ground in large numbers in a relatively few well-defined regions of the world; they have been thought, by some, to be the remains of thunderbolts.

Mythology aside, however, tektites were the subject of intense scientific speculation throughout much of the twentieth century because of their unknown origins and suspected extraterrestrial connections. They have an unusual chemical composition, high in silica, and are totally unlike any of the known, terrestrial, volcanic glasses, or any material of meteoritic origin. The majority of them are spherical in shape, but there are also oblate spheroids, now and then a dumbbell, and a few teardrops, discs or cylinders. They are known on every continent except Antarctica and South America, and occur in distinct geographical zones known as *strewn fields*; they have formed at widely different times over the Earth's history, and appear, from dating techniques and other evidence, to have fallen from the sky in geologically fairly recent times.

So where did they come from, these mysterious little spheres and cylinders of unfamiliar crystal? They were assumed to be of extraterrestrial origin, since some tektites contain bubbles of vapour at a very low atmospheric pressure, equivalent to that some 18 miles above the Earth. There were theories that they might have come from ancient volcanic eruptions on the Moon, but analysis of lunar rock brought back by the Apollo missions ruled this out. And in any event, they do not appear to have suffered any cosmic-ray bombardment, as would be expected if they had spent some time in space.

It is well accepted now that tektites were originally fragments of terrestrial rock, liquefied and blasted from the ground by the impact of a meteorite, to sail high into the atmosphere and fall to Earth again – a consequence of a kind of meteoric splash. Interestingly, late in the twentieth century a new strewn-field was discovered covering the western Caribbean and the eastern part of Mexico, whose tektites were found to date from 64.5 million years ago; if they do indeed comprise debris from a massive asteroid collision with the Earth, their existence supports the theory that a high-energy impact of this kind may have been responsible for the many mass extinctions and total demise of the dinosaurs around that time.

Dirk Wiersma, *These tektites were found on the Indonesian Isle of Billiton, and so are called Billitonites.*
Science Photo Library

Why the Walls Came Tumbling Down

31 March 2005

Jericho in biblical times, like many places in our own day, had serious problems with 'anti-social behaviour', and even 'criminality'. It was there, you may remember, that the good Samaritan had to come to the rescue of 'a certain man who went down from Jerusalem to Jericho, and fell among thieves'. But then the place had had a nasty history, which may well have induced traumatic stress in some of its inhabitants. Some years previously, Joshua had been given a mandate by the Lord to take possession of the Promised Land, and in fulfilment of this mission he led the Israelites across the Jordan; he advanced on the fortified city of Jericho – 'and the walls came tumbling down'.

The Bible clearly blames the Lord for this timely demolition. 'Go round about the city, with all ye fighting men once a day': he allegedly instructed Joshua, 'so shall ye do for six days. And on the seventh day the priests shall take the seven trumpets . . . and shall walk before the ark of the covenant: And the priests shall sound the trumpets, and when they shall sound a long blast, all the people shall shout together with a very great shout, and the walls of the city shall fall to the ground.'

And so, allegedly, it happened. But scientists like to hypothesise about the methodologies the Lord employs in achieving such Biblical objectives. In the case of Jericho, they think it might have been an earthquake.

Earthquakes, apparently, are rather common in the neighbourhood. Jericho lies on the Dead Sea Rift, a fault that runs north-south through Palestine and down into the Red Sea. In terms of plate tectonics, the rift is a boundary between the 'Arabian' plate to the east and the 'African-Sinai' plate to the west, and the two move relative to each other at an average speed approaching one centimetre every year. But the movement is erratic; rather than sliding smoothly past each other, the plates periodically relieve the built-up stress in 'jerks' that are palpable as seismic tremors.

More than 30 major earthquakes have been documented in the vicinity of the Dead Sea in the last 2,000 years, the most recent one in 1927, and the walls of Jericho have collapsed several times in the city's 10,000-year history. Moreover, evidence that Joshua's entrance to the city was facilitated in this way is enhanced by the additional information in the Bible that the flow of the river Jordan was cut off at the same time.

Such disruptions, typically lasting for one or two days, have been recorded in 1160, 1267, 1546, 1834 and 1906 – always in association with seismic activity in the region.

The coincidence of the sudden destruction of the walls of Jericho with the interruption of the Jordan waters leaves scientists in little doubt as to how the Lord contributed to Joshua's achievement.

Ms Fr 247 f.89 The Fall of Jericho, illustration from 'Antiquités Judaïques', c.1470 (vellum), **Jean Fouquet (c.1420–80) and Studio**
Bibliothèque Nationale, Paris, France/The Bridgeman Art Library

A Very Capable Hans

2 April 2005

Hans Christian Andersen, by all accounts, was unattractive. He grew from a shy, sickly, ugly child into a gauche, unprepossessing adult, a manic-depressive egomaniac and a hypochondriac beset by phobias. But, my goodness, he could write! In his early years he penned six novels and some 30 full-length plays, all of them long since forgotten, but 160 fairy tales, written between 1835 and 1872, were to bring him world renown, even in his lifetime. In Europe in the late nineteenth century, the sales of his books were exceeded only by the Bible.

Andersen was born to poor and dysfunctional parents in the Danish port of Odense 200 years ago today, on 2 April 1805. At the age of 14 he went to Copenhagen to try his hand at acting, a craft at which he failed. At 23 he turned his hand to writing, and before his 40th birthday he was famous.

We are, all of us, familiar since childhood with many of his tales. Who can forget 'The Ugly Duckling', which seems to have been a wistful metaphor for Andersen himself? Who has not searched in vain for a wholesome moral in the violent mayhem of 'The Tinder Box'? And have we not all been thrilled by the strange surrealism of 'The Snow Queen' and moved to tears by the pathos of 'The Little Mermaid'? Whatever the story, Andersen's prose flows effortlessly on from page to page, lyrical description weaving in and out, forever changing place with stark, cold narrative.

His meteorological depiction, as you might expect, is quite superb. Before the Little Mermaid meets her Prince, for example, 'the sea became restless, and a moaning, grumbling sound could be heard beneath the surface. Heavy clouds darkened the sky, and lightning appeared in the distance. The waves rose mountains high, as if they would have overtopped the mast, but the ship dived like a swan between them, and then rose again on their lofty, foaming crests.'

Elsewhere, a summer thunderstorm provides the climax to 'The Story of the Year': 'Dark clouds gathered, which in wavy outlines of black and indigo piled themselves up like mountains, higher and higher. They came from every side, and then swooped towards the forest, where every sound had been silenced as if by magic, every breath hushed, every bird mute. All nature stood still in grave suspense.

'And then came a flash of light, flaming, burning, all-devouring, after which

From The Little Mermaid,
(watercolour)
Harry Clarke (1889–1931)
National Gallery of Ireland

darkness returned amid a rolling crash of thunder. The rain poured down in streams, while the corn and the blades of grass lay beaten down and swamped, so that it seemed impossible that they should ever raise themselves again.'

Hans Christian Andersen never married, although it is said that he proposed to at least three women during his lifetime. He was refused, presumably, on grounds of looks, or temperament, or both. He died, aged 70, in 1875.

Making the Best of April Showers

5 April 2005

April can be a charlatan; one might almost say a hypocrite. It has the reputation of being a very gentle month, with its longer days, its higher temperatures, its daffodils and its emerging greenery, all calculated to induce in unwary souls a premature complacency about advancing spring. But April showers, as we have seen in recent days, are a reality and often vicious; we have had to cope with what Proteus, Shakespeare's lovesick gentleman of Verona, called:

> *The uncertain glory of an April day,*
> *Which now shows all the beauty of the sun,*
> *And by and by a cloud takes all away!*

Now, what should you do when faced with a sudden April shower? Should you run helter-skelter to the nearest shelter, thereby suffering a soaking down the front? Or should you take your time, encountering fewer raindrops in any given interval, but enduring the whole unpleasantness for rather longer? Which option, in the end, leaves an individual less wet? The issue is as old as homo sapiens, at least, and dates from the time when some distant ancestor first had the bright idea of rising on his or her hind legs and walking upright.

Some years ago, dedicated meteorologists at the University of Reading researched the problem in considerable detail. They assumed, for the purpose of their argument, that the rain was falling vertically, and that its intensity was constant over time. Moreover, to simplify their calculations, they approximated the average person by an imaginary rectangular block of appropriate dimensions. Clearly, a person-block at rest, when exposed to a vertical downpour, will have the rain impacting directly on its horizontal surfaces; if, on the other hand, it moves, it will also collide with any raindrops in its way. The researchers worked out the total quantity of water encountered by this person-block as it moved at various speeds, over given distances, and for a variety of different rates of rainfall. The answers are very interesting indeed.

Obviously, if the subject of this experiment stands still, he gets very wet indeed because the rain falls down on him indefinitely. But if he moves, the total amount of water encountered turns out to decrease rapidly as he increases his rate of progress to a brisk walk – for the simple reason that the faster he travels, the quicker he reaches shelter. But, surprisingly perhaps, beyond a brisk walk, any further increase in speed has very little effect on how wet he gets; if he runs like mad, he will reach shelter very quickly, but at this higher speed he collects more raindrops on the way, and consequently experiences a more serious wetting down the front.

The best tactic, it seems, is to head for the shelter at precisely six miles per hour, or slightly more than walking pace. If you move more slowly than that, you will catch more rain – and going faster is of no benefit at all.

L'Averse (The Downpour), 1893
(oil on canvas),
Paul Serusier (1863–1927),
Musée d'Orsay, Paris/© RMN/
Hervé Lewandowski

Poetry's Loss and Science's Gain

7 April 2005

'He was not at all a loquacious man. Nor was he one who seemed inclined to approach with any degree of intimacy those of whom he knew a good deal, but at the same time one who met every advance on the part of others with a ready and attractive affability. Other men did not seem necessary to him, or to the existence of his happiness, so that his sympathy with the happiness and sorrow, the good and ill, of the whole creation as it discovers itself in his poetry gave one the feeling of his natural character being very peculiar.'

This perceptive pen-picture of William Wordsworth, written in the 1830s by Eliza Hamilton, sister of the mathematician and astronomer William Rowan Hamilton, was based on impressions gleaned by her during one of the poet's several trips to Ireland to visit Hamilton at Dunsink Observatory.

Today, as it happens, is the 235th anniversary of Wordsworth's birth, he having first seen the light of day at Cockermouth in Cumberland on 7 April 1770. Although he travelled widely, even spending a short spell in Paris during the Reign of Terror, the poet passed most of his life in his beloved Lake District. In 1813 he settled at Rydal Mount, a house two miles from Grasmere, where he lived until his death in 1850.

Much of Wordsworth's prolific output reflects the climate and the weather of the Lake District – often, it must be said, in somewhat maudlin terms. In 'Lucy Grey', for example, he tells the story of a fatality in a moorland snowstorm:

> *The storm came on before its time,*
> *She wandered up and down,*
> *And many a hill did Lucy climb*
> *But never reached the Town.*

Now, you might think poor Lucy rather unfortunate to be caught out like this, but in Wordsworth's time that sort of nasty weather seemed to occur quite often in those parts. He warns us in 'The Brothers' that:

Portrait of William
Wordsworth
James Bromley, after Sir
William Boxall
photos.com

*. . . a sharp Maystorm
Will come with loads of January snow,
And in one night send twenty score of sheep
To feed the ravens. . .*

Clearly, of William Wordsworth it could be said, as Rossini remarked of Richard Wagner, that 'he has lovely moments, but awful quarters of an hour'. But at least Wordsworth may have made a valuable contribution to our Irish scientific heritage.

The poet and William Rowan Hamilton first met at Keswick in 1827 and formed an instant and lasting friendship, despite the 35-year difference in their ages. During the decade that followed, Wordsworth stayed with Hamilton at Dunsink on three occasions, and it was on one of these visits that he advised the young Hamilton, despite the latter's ambitions in that direction, that he would never succeed in being a poet of any consequence. Thus discouraged, Hamilton largely abandoned poetry and went on to become perhaps the greatest mathematician Ireland has produced.

Machismo in the Rain

8 April 2005

'I was born,' wrote Robinson Crusoe through the pen of Daniel Defoe, 'in the year 1632, in the city of York, of a good family, though not of that country, my father being a foreigner of Bremen, who had settled first at Hull.' Young Robinson, as we know, inherited his father's wanderlust, and as a consequence became the archetypal desert island castaway.

Now Crusoe kept himself busy during his adventure, and one of his numerous inventions he describes as follows: 'After this I spent a great deal of time and pains to make me an umbrella. I was indeed in great want of one, and had a great mind to make one. I had seen them made in the Brazils, where they are very useful in the great heats which are there; and I felt the heats every jot as great here, and greater too, being nearer to the equinox. Besides, as I was obliged to be much abroad, it was a most useful thing to me, as well for the rains as for the heats.'

The use of umbrellas, in the guise of parasols, had evolved in Britain during the seventeenth and early eighteenth centuries as an essential out-door accessory for any well-dressed lady, and by 1710 Jonathan Swift could describe how

> *The tuck'd-up seamstress walks with hasty strides,*
> *While streams run down her oiled umbrella's sides.*

The unusual thing about Robinson Crusoe's narrative, however, is that in 1719, when the story was published, still less in the 1660s when the action of the tale takes place, no self-respecting male would have dared to carry this device; an umbrella was as feminine in its implications, and in its limitations as to use, as were a petticoat or farthingale.

The first man to have used one in these parts is said to have been a Londoner called Jonas Hanway. Around 1750, to the great amusement of his fellow citizens, he began to carry an umbrella to ward off the rain. The populace did not spare his finer feelings; the more dignified members of society would poke gentle fun in his direction, the common folk were more vociferous, and small boys along his route would pelt the brave eccentric with putrid vegetables and rotten eggs.

Hanway persevered, but in fact it took many years for the manly use of the umbrella to become the norm. Even by 1815, the year that saw the Battle of Waterloo, there was only one umbrella in the whole of Cambridge, owned by a shop and rented by the hour. In due course inns and coffee houses began to keep one for the protection of customers going to and from their carriages, and by the end of the nineteenth century the umbrella had become an indispensable personal protector against the whims and sorrows of our outrageous climate.

Jonas Hanway Pioneers the First Umbrella in London, 19th-century engraving

A Multitude of Mills

16 April 2005

In the Great Storm that ravaged the south of England on the night of 26–27 November 1703, 400 windmills were wrecked, many of them because the intense friction generated by the rapidly rotating blades had caused them to catch fire. Now, what might surprise many people about this statistic is that there were 400 windmills actually extant in England at the time.

But the number was very much greater. The earliest recorded windmill in Britain dates from 1191, and at their peak there are reckoned to have been over 10,000 of them at work, used mainly for grinding corn and for drainage. In Holland in 1750 there were 8,000 windmills, and in northern Germany around 20,000 at that time.

The earliest machines for grinding corn drew their motive power from a long horizontal beam which was pulled around and around in a circular path by animals, or even by a man. Samson, you may recall, ended up in this unfortunate position; having foolishly confided to Delilah the secret of his *haute coiffure*, he found himself severely debilitated, handed over to the Philistines, and ultimately, according to Milton's version:

> *Betray'd, Captiv'd, and both my eyes put out,*
> *Made of my enemies the scorn and gaze; . . .*
> *Eyeless in Gaza, at the mill with slaves.*

A later version of the same idea was the treadmill, driven by treading or walking on vanes or paddles to turn a horizontal shaft. In due course, water was substituted for foot-power with the development of the water-mill, and the height of automation was reached, still many centuries BC, when wind began to be used for this purpose.

The traditional windmill, with wooden or canvas sails on a horizontal axis, was introduced to western Europe by the returning Crusaders in the twelfth century. Early examples had no arrangement for turning the sails into the wind, and were simply built to face into what seemed to be the most advantageous direction. This disadvantage was overcome in later models by mounting the entire mill on a post on which it could rotate – a 'post-mill' – the orientation being carried out manually by means of a 'tail-pole' fitted to the structure. Finally, in the fourteenth century, the 'tower mill' evolved; it had a fixed body – the tower – surmounted by a rotatable 'cap' on to which the sails were fixed.

Dozens of such tower-mills were built in Ireland in the eighteenth and early nineteenth centuries. By that time they incorporated clever automatic devices to keep the sails facing the wind – the most important being the 'fantail' invented in 1745 by Edmund Lee. The fan remained edge-on to the wind and motionless whenever the windmill was correctly orientated; if, however, the wind changed direction, the fantail began to rotate, operating a system of gears which rotated the whole cap to bring the sails back into the wind again.

Dutch Windmills, 1884 (oil on canvas), **Eugène Boudin (1824–98),**
Musée de la Chartreuse, Douai

The Pope and the Weather

20 April 2005

It is of no relevance to this column whether Pope Benedict XVI be arch-conservative or liberal. His reign – almost to coin a pun – will be judged purely on meteorological, not theological, criteria, and as yet we have heard little of his views on weather matters.

He does, however, have heavy weather-baggage with him, since his eponym, St. Benedict, has much the same reputation in France as Swithin does a little farther north. Every Frenchman knows that if it rains on Benedict's feastday, 21 March, rain is guaranteed for each of the succeeding 40 days.

But some Popes, over the centuries, have given meteorology a helping hand. In the case of Pope Nicholas I in the ninth century it was inadvertent, and came about when he decreed that the figure of a cock should surmount the topmost pinnacle of every abbey, cathedral and parish church in Christendom. The emblem was intended, of course, to recall St. Peter's weakness; having denied the Lord three times, Peter heard the crowing of a cock and was reminded of his Master's forecast – whereupon, we are told, the repentant apostle 'went out and wept bitterly'. But, in due course, the papal ordinance was harnessed to the benefit of meteorology by mediaeval architects, who used the 'weathercock' to show the wind's direction.

Gregory XIII inherited St. Peter's Chair in 1572, and is probably best remembered for his reform of the old Julian Calendar. His initiative resulted in what ought to have been 5 October 1582, becoming 15 October, a jump which removed an error that had accumulated over 1,500 years. But meteorologists remember Gregory as the founder in 1578 of the Tower of the Winds in the Vatican, the region's first weather-observing station.

Papal meteorology flowered most, however, during the long reign of Pope Pius IX from 1846 to 1878. Pius had a far-sighted view of the value of international scientific co-operation, and with the help of a Jesuit, Father Angelo Secchi, Director of the Pontifical Observatory at the Roman College, Pius established a wide network of weather stations throughout the Papal States.

Pius's successor, Leo XIII, is best remembered as the author of the social encyclical *Rerum Novarum*. But in another promulgation, *Ut Mysticam*, issued on

14 March 1891, Leo furthered Vatican meteorology by establishing a new Pontifical Astronomical and Meteorological Observatory in Rome, to be called the Specola Vaticana.

The Specola, as it is called, remained in Rome until the early 1930s, and then moved to a better site at Castel Gandolfo, some distance from the city. There it still operates, 1,200 feet above sea level on the rim of the crater containing Lake Albano. Its altitude, combined with its clear view across the Roman campagna to the western horizon some 50 miles away, makes it very suitable for meteorological and astronomical pursuits.

St Benedict, 1441 (fresco),
Fra Angelico (c.1387–1455)
Wikipedia Commons

The Secret of Turner's Skies

23 April 2005

Joseph Mallord William Turner was a barber's son, and throughout his long life was forever secretive, unsociable and quite eccentric. Unable to write even the shortest letter without innumerable grammatical mistakes, he nonetheless became England's greatest landscape painter, described by the influential critic John Ruskin as 'unfathomable in knowledge, solitary in power, sent as a prophet to reveal to men the mysteries of the universe'. He was, in a word, a genius.

Turner was born 230 years ago today, on 23 April 1775. He was a mere stripling of a lad when he painted *Buttermere Lake, with part of Cromackwater – a Shower* in the late 1790s, and had yet to adopt his unconventional and somewhat controversial later style. But a keen meteorological eye can be discerned. *Buttermere* portrays a lakeland scene on a dark and sombre day, and is dominated by a perfect rainbow, the spectral colours of which, with red on the outside, are accurately portrayed. Moreover, clearly visible outside the primary bow is the not uncommon secondary rainbow, and there is also a reflected rainbow – what appears to be a portion of the primary arc reflected from the surface of the lake below.

But as time went by, Turner began to imbue his work with an exuberant, romantic turbulence, an idiosyncrasy which came to be widely recognised, and which, combined with his penchant for a long title, led *Punch* to suggest that he might consider painting *A Typhoon bursting over the Whirlpool of a Norwegian Maelstrom, with a Ship on fire, an Eclipse, and a pendant Lunar Rainbow.*

He became remarkable, too, for the vivid, almost lurid, quality of his later skies, as, for example, in the spectacular sunrise of *Ulysses Deriding Polyphemus*, the clouded sunset in *The Fighting Temeraire*, and the flaming yellow sky in *The Arch of Constantine in Rome.* His colours became even more extravagant as the nineteenth century progressed, but it has been suggested that they were less idiosyncratic, and perhaps more representational, than has been commonly thought. Distant volcanoes may have been the cause.

After a lull in volcanic activity between 1783 and 1802, a series of eruptions in the early decades of the new century threw vast quantities of dust into the stratosphere. Dust like this has the effect, when the Sun is near to the horizon, of filtering out the blue part of the spectrum from the sunlight with great effectiveness; this would have allowed the colours red and orange to predominate at sunset to a much greater extent than is the case today. This volcanic dust, some argue, may in part explain the rich flamboyance of Joseph Turner's skies.

Famous, eccentric, rich and more secretive than ever, Turner spent his last years in diminishing health, living in Chelsea. He died in December 1851, and is buried in St. Paul's Cathedral.

The Fighting Temeraire, 1839 (oil on canvas), **Joseph Mallord William Turner (1775–1851)**
National Gallery, London, UK/The Bridgeman Art Library

The Moon and the Weather

27 April 2005

You may have noticed that the Moon was full of late, a circumstance which concentrates the mind most wonderfully. On this occasion, it reminded me of the oft-quoted rhyme, which epitomises current meteorological wisdom about lunar influences on earthly weather:

> *The moon and the weather may change together,*
> *But a change of the moon does not change the weather;*
> *If we'd no moon at all, and that may seem strange,*
> *We still would have weather that's subject to change.*

Like nearly all epitomes, it is not entirely true.

Take the first two lines. Despite what they assert, it has been discovered that the average temperature of the Earth actually rises and falls ever so slightly during a lunar month, oscillating over a range of 0.02 of a °C as the Moon waxes and wanes. This variation can be traced to the *pas de deux* performed together by the Earth and Moon as they travel side by side in space.

The gravity that holds the Moon in thrall also exerts an attractive force on the Earth itself, tending to disturb it from its solar orbit. Rather than thinking of the Moon as revolving around the Earth, we should more properly regard both bodies as orbiting around their joint centre of mass, which is close to, but not exactly at, the centre of the Earth. Viewed in this light, as the Earth-Moon combination rotates in space, the Earth moves slightly closer to the Sun than it ought to be at full Moon, and slightly farther away when the system has swung through 180 degrees to the new-Moon phase. The difference is a mere 9,000 miles, but enough to account for some, at least, of the observed increase in temperature when the Moon is full.

And then we have the last two lines – 'no Moon at all'. The axis of rotation of the Earth, as we know, is 'tilted' at an angle of about 23 degrees to the plane of the planet's orbit around the Sun, and it is this 'obliquity of the ecliptic', as astronomers like to call it, that gives us the seasons.

But the obliquity of the ecliptic is not constant. It varies from about 25 degrees to 22 degrees and back again over a period of some 40,000 years, the so-called 'Milankovitch Cycle', which influences the comings and the goings of ice ages over the millennia. Moreover, we have the Moon to thank for the fact that the variation in the axial tilt is a mere 2.6 degrees. Computer simulations suggest that without the Moon's torque, the Earth would wobble chaotically on its axis, like a spinning top in the course of slowing down. Without the Moon, the axial tilt would vary widely, increasing at times to as much as 50 degrees, and the Earth would lurch irregularly from unimaginable ice ages to searing interglacial heatwaves.

Photograph of the Earth and the Moon, from Space
NASA

The Witches' Holocaust

30 April 2005

Tonight, the eve of May Day or Walpurgisnacht, is seen as evil in many parts of Europe. It was believed that on this night witches and other evil creatures of the occult were free to roam the world and cast their nasty spells on poor defenceless people in their villages. In high and lonely places 'midnight shout and revelry and tipsie dance' took place as 12 of the most wicked formed a 'coven', and led the celebration of a Witches' Sabbath.

Of course, there are no witches now; as Yeats tells us:

All the wild witches, those most noble ladies,
For all their broom-sticks and their tears,
Their angry tears, are gone.

Part of the reason for this, one might conclude, may be that they have been exterminated. In any event, between 1200 and around 1750 as many as a million individuals in Europe were executed for the crime of witchcraft, the majority of the trials and executions taking place during the sixteenth and seventeenth centuries. Although originally an outcome of the Inquisition, the witchcraft trials in due course became ubiquitous, conducted by both ecclesiastical and secular courts, and by both Catholics and Protestants; the victims were primarily women, mainly poor, and disproportionately widows.

Now, an interesting weather-angle on these witchcraft trials has been unearthed by Harvard graduate student Emily Oster in a paper 'Witchcraft, Weather and Economic Growth in Renaissance Europe' published in *The Journal of Economic Perspectives*. Oster noted that the peak in the frequency of witchcraft trials coincided closely with the very cold period in European climatic history referred to as the Little Ice Age, a period when temperatures were a degree or more below today's norms. Analysing the relevant data, decade by decade from 1520 to 1770, Oster found a significant relationship, throughout Europe, between average local temperature and the number of persons put on trial for witchcraft. When the temperature dropped for a decade or two, the number of trials consistently increased; by contrast, during relatively warmer periods, witchcraft trials were significantly fewer.

Oster's thesis is that during periods of exceptional cold, when crop yields were low, famines common and times generally very hard, the people found their scapegoats in those unfortunate creatures whom they identified as witches. Nor was there any doubt about the power of witches to engineer social calamity of this kind. In the Papal Bull that accompanied *Malleus Malleficarum – the vade mecum*, published in 1484, on how witches should be treated, Pope Innocent VIII wrote, 'It has lately come to our ears ... [that] many persons of both sexes ... have blasted the produce of the earth, the grapes of the vine, the fruits of trees, together with orchards, meadows, corn, wheat and other cereals.' And the *Malleus* itself has a chapter entitled 'How they Raise and Stir up Hailstorms and Tempests, and Cause Lightning to Blast both Men and Beasts.'

Walpurgisnacht (Night of the Witches), 1946 (oil on canvas),
Ary Stillman (1891–1967), Indianapolis Museum of Art
Gift of the Stillman-Lack Foundation

The Climate of King Arthur's Avalon

2 May 2005

Then saw they how there hove a dusky barge,
Dark as a funeral scarf from stem to stern,
Beneath them;

This was Sir Bedivere's fourth visit to the lake within an hour. Twice, you may recall from *Morte d'Arthur*, he had gone to the shore to return Excalibur to where it belonged, and twice had hidden it. But on his third visit, he cast the magic sword into the lake, from which an arm, 'clothed in white samite, mystic, wonderful', arose and caught it by the hilt. And now, on this, his fourth visit, Bedivere carried the dying Arthur to the barge which would take him on his last journey to the island-valley of Avilion.

It was a most delightful spot, this Avilion, a place, according to Arthur:

Where falls not hail, or rain, or any snow,
Nor ever wind blows loudly; but it lies
Deep-meadow'd, happy, fair with orchard-lawns
And bowery hollows crown'd with summer sea ...

The lake itself may well have helped make Avilion idyllic. Water acts like a giant storage heater, responding only very slowly to changes in the temperature of its surroundings. A good-sized area of deep water, therefore, tends to moderate the local climate, protecting it from the extremes to which it might otherwise be subject. The moderating influence of the water would render the island-valley's deep meadows and orchard-lawns much less subject to frost in winter than might be the case elsewhere.

On a hot summer's day, the air over a deep lake remains relatively cold compared to the surrounding countryside, and so a gentle cooling 'lake breeze', like a miniature sea breeze, develops to waft lightly onto the adjacent land. Air that moves shorewards in this way is generally rich in moisture, and enhances any clouds tending to form some distance inland from the shoreline. But the shore-bound lake air must be replaced by air sinking down towards the centre of the lake from higher levels in the atmosphere, so lakes tend to be areas of subsidence in summer. And consequently – since clouds are associated with rising rather than sinking air – the summer skies above Avilion on its large expanse of water would remain relatively cloud-free and sunny compared to the surrounding countryside.

This effect is particularly noticeable in spring and early summer, when any rise in temperature experienced by the water lags far behind that of the adjacent land. In autumn and winter, however, these processes are reversed; cold nights produce the opposite effect to warm sunny days, with a light current of cool air drifting out onto the surface of the lake to replace any relatively warmer air over the water that might have succumbed to a tendency to float upwards. The upward-moving air over a lake in winter, however, produces a tendency for greater average cloudiness, and a layer of cloud provides additional protection against winter frosts.

Sunrise Mist, Ontario, Canada
Pavel Chaiko, *photos.com*

Two Sides of William Rowan Hamilton

3 May 2005

'Please do a piece,' a regular reader of this column wrote, 'on William Rowan Hamilton. He is on the new 48-cent stamp, and very few people have any notion who he was.'

'Done that!' I mumbled to myself. But then came the merest shadow of a doubt, which grew and grew. Driven, in the end, to consult my *Index pro Temporibus Hibernicis Scriptorum*, I discovered not a single *Weather Eye* on William Hamilton. Here goes!

Sir William Rowan Hamilton was perhaps the greatest mathematician and scientist Ireland has produced. He is topical at present because he was born 200 years ago this year, precisely at midnight, we are told, on 4–5 August 1805. His father, Archibald, was a Dublin lawyer, but William's mentor in his formative years was his uncle, Rev. James Hamilton, who was a curate of Trim in County Meath. Uncle James provided William's early education; by the age of five the lad was fluent in Latin, Greek and Hebrew, and at 15 he was fully conversant with the mathematical works of luminaries like Newton and Laplace, even to the point of finding fault with their conclusions.

Hamilton studied at Trinity College Dublin and graduated with high honours in 1827. But more importantly, in his final year at college he presented a paper at the Royal Irish Academy, *An Account of a Theory of Systems of Rays*, which was acknowledged at the time as the best paper ever received by the Academy. On the strength of this and his general reputation, William Hamilton was appointed Astronomer Royal for Ireland, Andrews Professor of Astronomy at Trinity, and third Director of Dunsink Observatory. He was only 21, and he was to hold the professorship and live at the Observatory until his death.

Hamilton made contributions to algebra, mechanics, geometry and optics important enough to give him a European reputation at an early age, and sufficient to earn him a knighthood by the age of 30. But he is best remembered for devising the mathematical concept of 'quaternions'. Cathartic inspiration for the notion came to him one day in October 1843 while walking with his wife along the towpath of the Royal Canal, where on one of the stones of the nearby Brougham Bridge he famously inscribed the formula.

But there was a poignant, less successful side to William Hamilton. The love of his young life, Catherine Disney, accepted the hand of another man in marriage, and Hamilton never quite recovered from the disappointment. His own subsequent marriage was not particularly happy, nor was he contented in his work as an astronomer; indeed, the traditional activities at Dunsink Observatory progressed, at best, in a routine manner during his lengthy tenure. His middle and later years were marred by a weakness for alcoholic drink, to which he frequently, and sometimes publicly, succumbed. He died at Dunsink from a severe attack of gout in September 1865.

Portrait of **William Rowan Hamilton**
Autotype from photograph taken in 1857, Fulneck, Yorkshire
Library of Congress

The Day that Ladybirds Rose Up in Protest

6 May 2005

'Population,' Thomas Malthus pointed out 200 years ago, 'increases in a geometrical ratio when it is left unchecked,' and his simple observation has been a source of worry to us ever since. Moreover, as every gardener knows, green-fly and other aphids are enthusiastic followers of Malthus; indeed someone, somewhere, once calculated that a mere ten generations bred from a single aphid, assuming all survived, would collectively weigh in at almost 40 tonnes.

Fortunately for us, not all survive, and so aphids have not quite inherited the earth. Ladybirds, for one thing, do their best to eat as many as they can, and the weather, too, puts a periodic brake on population growth.

Aphids, for one thing, are very sensitive to cold. This is not to say that in this respect they are particularly fragile creatures; some species can survive a temperature of –20°C, but nevertheless, sub-zero temperatures typically decimate a population, and even a slight frost severely limits their ability to move. If an aphid cannot move, it cannot reach its food, and quickly dies.

On the other hand, an explosion of the aphid population often occurs when a mild winter is followed by a warm spring. Reproduction continues through the winter months, so numbers increase unless checked by freezing temperatures. The importance of a warm spring lies in the fact that the insects need to migrate to sources of new food at that time of year, and flight is not possible for them unless the temperature climbs to well over 10°C. A few warm days in early spring, however, give the aphids early access to abundant food, and this in turn facilitates their future reproduction.

When things get really bad, all we can do is depend on the ladybirds. With a bumper crop of aphids, ladybirds can feast in early summer to their hearts' delight, and their numbers, too, may sometimes multiply to plague proportions. The most memorable year in this respect was 1976, one of the longest, hottest summers of recent times. Most of the previous season's ladybirds had survived the mild winter, and then a wet spring encouraged a lush growth of vegetation, which in turn produced a glut of the ladybird's favourite food.

Thomas Malthus, 1833, John Linnell (1792–1882).
By permission of the Master of Haileybury and ISC.

But then a famine followed. By midsummer most of the aphids had been eaten up; worse still, the plants on which they thrived had shrivelled in the scorching heat, and this wiped out nearly all those aphids that were left. By the end of July every ladybird in Britain and Ireland was threatened with starvation, and in due course they staged something very like a protest march. Some of you may remember that in the early days of August that year, billions of ladybirds took to the air in search of food and travelled up to 400 miles until they reached the sea. They then made a well-publicised descent en masse on several crowded beaches in the east of England.

Heaven has Begun for Corrib Trout

7 May 2005

L'*Enfer, c'est les Autres*, declared Jean Paul Sartre: 'Hell is other people!' And at the other end of the scale, no doubt each one's concept of their own particular Heaven is equally subjective. Rupert Brooke, however, took the idea a step further and tried to imagine what Heaven for a trout would look like:

> *Fat caterpillars drift around,*
> *And Paradisal grubs are found,*
> *Unfading moths, immortal flies,*
> *And the worm that never dies.*

The nearest approach in real life to this fishy Nirvana occurs in late spring with the annual 'rise' of the mayfly. Heaven in this case is ephemeral; the flies, far from being immortal, have a lifespan of only a few days. But during the rise the trout enjoys a rare abundance of what seems to be its favourite food.

The mayfly nymph spends a year or two uneventfully buried in the mud or sand at the bottom of a lake or river. It emerges with the rise into the open air with millions of its fellows, undergoing a series of metamorphoses to become the adult mayfly, a large insect about two inches long, with semi-transparent lemon-coloured wings.

Now, adult mayflies have a brief but very pleasant life; their entire energy is exclusively devoted to mating on the wing. This they do in dense and feverish swarms, the objective in the case of any individual often being achieved within an hour or two. Almost immediately the female deposits her eggs into the river or pond, and very shortly afterwards she and her recent paramour collapse exhausted on the surface of the water, where they expire with wings outstretched in a classic *dénouement* worthy of the great Fonteyn.

This brief sojourn above the water takes place dramatically each spring, and as the insect's name implies, very often in the month of May. And this year, according to one of Joe Duffy's callers the other day on *Liveline*, the mayfly has already risen on the Corrib. The reason why, as always, is elusive.

The Lock on the Stour (oil on canvas), Unknown, after John Constable
Anglesey Abbey, The Fairhaven Collection (The National Trust). © National Trust Images

The accepted wisdom is that mild, dry, sunny weather brings an early rise: this may be because the water temperature is high. Alternatively, it may depend on sunshine heating the silt of the shallow waters where the larvae grow. Or the sunshine may help the growth of algae, which provides the food and brings about an early hatch; or yet again, it may be rain-related, since low rainfall means lower water levels, leaving the water rich in nourishment.

Whatever the reason, the annual rise of the mayfly provides tasty morsels for many a waiting trout. The rise also provides an annual 'happy hour' for anglers, since the fish, jumping repeatedly from the water in their eagerness to catch the mayfly, are undiscerning in their enthusiasm. And, sadly for the trout, one vital ingredient of Rupert Brooke's fishy Heaven is missing: 'Oh! never fly conceals a hook'.

The Elusive Sweetness of a Stradivarius

9 May 2005

There is a wooded Alpine region to the north of the Italian town of Brescia which is known, I have been told, as the Forest of the Violins. Tradition has it that it was from here in the seventeenth and early eighteenth centuries that the renowned violin-makers of Cremona would obtain the wood from which to make their instruments. The most talented of these artisans was one Antonio Stradivari, born in 1644, who produced more than a thousand stringed instruments between 1665 and his death in 1737. Some 650 of them are still extant, and everyone agrees that they represent the ultimate perfection of the craft.

The exact reason for the unusual sweetness of a Stradivarius has proved elusive. The superior tone is sometimes attributed to the method of assembly of the instrument, or to the quantity and nature of the varnish used; others try to explain it in terms of special qualities inherent in the wood itself, and here the weather may have played a part.

In mediaeval times, Europe had enjoyed a comparatively benign climate, but a sudden change took place in the middle of the sixteenth century. It grew significantly colder, and the period from about 1600 to 1850, with average temperatures more than a degree below today's norms, was the coldest for 12,000 years. In Switzerland and the Nordic countries the glaciers advanced over areas of fertile farmland, and did not retreat again until the middle of the nineteenth century. The winters were long and very severe, the summers cold and wet, and contemporary accounts show that March was regarded as a winter month. The growing season was four to six weeks shorter than it is now, and the weather was often extremely variable; harvest expectations often went unrealised, and this contributed to social unrest. This period is remembered as the Little Ice Age.

Now, the part of the Little Ice Age covering Stradivari's lifetime was particularly harsh, and during the long winters and cool summers trees experienced a rate of growth which was much slower than the norm. This was particularly so at relatively high altitudes, so that the spruce trees harvested from the Forest of the Violins around this time for making musical instruments had tree rings that were exceptionally narrow. Examination of the wood of Stradivari's violins have shown the wood in some of them to have something like 220 tree rings over a distance of 15cm or so, compared to the 90 to 150 that might be the norm and which is evident on modern violins. The result was a very dense wood, and some experts argue that this resonates acoustically much better than does 'ordinary' wood.

But none of this explains why the instruments made by Stradivari were so seductively sweeter than those of other contemporary Cremonese violin-makers who used wood from exactly the same source. This brings us back again to varnish and design.

The Violin, 1916 (oil on wood panel), **Juan Gris (1887–1927),** Kunstmuseum, Basle, Switzerland Giraudon/The Bridgeman Art Library

The Hues and Whys of Seas and Lakes

11 May 2005

The colour of any body of open water is to some extent determined by the sky. The water reflects the changing patterns of blue and white and grey above, and this alone can impart to it a wide variety of different tinges. But even under a relatively dark, uninteresting sky, the open sea exhibits a marked preponderance of blue compared to inland lakes.

For this there are many different reasons. A clue to their multiplicity can be found in the changing appearance of the sea itself – from season to season, day to day, and even hour to hour. The coastal shallows, moreover, are not the same colour as mid-ocean waters, and the appearance of both is quite different when viewed from a ship, as opposed to when looking down from an aircraft overhead. Indeed the appearance of the water depends not just on what you look at, but *when* you look at it and *how* you look at it as well.

The underlying phenomenon is the fact that water slowly absorbs any light that passes through it, and sea water absorbs the longer wavelengths of red and orange light more effectively than it absorbs the short, blue wavelengths; the sunlight is filtered, to leave it with a distinctly bluish tinge. Moreover, as the sunlight passes down into the depths, the tiny particles of liquid seawater obstruct some of the surviving blue light-waves and 'scatter' them back in the direction of the surface – there to emerge to be seen by an observer. So the white sunlight entering the sea is first filtered until it is predominantly blue, and then some of this blue light is scattered back in the direction of someone watching from above.

Now by the same mechanisms, the reflection of the sky may sometimes give a lake a whitish-blue appearance. More often, however, reflections of mountains and greenery around the shoreline impart a much darker colour to the water. But as in the case of the sea, the predominant colour of a lake is largely determined by light that has first penetrated the water and then been diverted upwards again in the direction of an observer.

The colour of this scattered light depends on the range of impurities suspended in the water, and the extent to which they affect the different wavelengths making up the sunlight. Very pure lakes often deliver a bluish tinge, just like the sea; increasing proportions of iron salts or humic acids result in scattered light that varies from light yellow to a darkish shade of brown. And sometimes, if the water is rich in large particles of peat washed down from surrounding bogs, the sunlight may be completely absorbed as it tries to penetrate the depths; no light at all remains to be scattered upwards and the lake takes on a black, rather sinister appearance.

La Grenouillère, 1869 (oil on canvas), **Claude Monet (1840–1926)**
Metropolitan Museum of Art, New York, USA/The Bridgeman Art Library

The First Knight of the Air

12 May 2005

'Some men,' says Shakespeare in *Twelfth Night*, 'are born great, some achieve greatness, and some have greatness thrust upon them.' Young Richard McGwire was firmly in the third category.

The thrust came 220 years ago today, on 12 May 1785, when McGwire, then a penniless 21-year-old student in his final term at Trinity College, went along to the square of what was to become Collins Barracks in Dublin to watch one Richard Crosbie ascend in a hydrogen balloon. Crosbie hoped that this would be the first crossing of the Irish Sea by air.

But neither fate nor avoirdupois were on the side of Mr. Crosbie. He was a substantial man, well over six feet tall and built to match, and when fully loaded up, the balloon was unable to raise the heavy aeronaut and his equipment from the ground. Rather than disappoint the large crowd, Crosbie invited the nearest suitable spectator to take his place. He chose the lithe McGwire.

With Richard McGwire on board, the balloon was successfully launched and drifted rapidly out over the Irish Sea. A poem, written in the aftermath to celebrate the great adventure, describes the atmosphere prevailing at the time:

> *Assembled thousands hail his venturous rise*
> *And watch his fate with reverential eyes;*
> *The clouds that with the lofty breezes fly,*
> *Seem to assist his swiftness through the sky.*

It was not to be a successful voyage. Over Ireland's Eye, the craft got into difficulties, and shortly afterwards landed in the sea several miles north-east of Howth. The hapless youth was flung into the water, and the poet calls upon the gods to save him:

Spread your mantles on the main;
Calm the pathless watery plain;
Watch the champion's swift descent
And guide the dangerous dire event;
And from encircling dismal death's alarms
Restore him to despairing Friendship's arms.

The gods duly obliged. McGwire managed to keep himself afloat for half an hour and was rescued by a boat from Howth. Despite its ignominious end, the adventure caught the imagination of the general public, and McGwire became the hero of the hour:

Make the dreadless youth renowned!
Spread his glorious name on high;
Let the wandering planets hear
How he spurned this lazy sphere!

And so it was that Richard McGwire was showered with honours. He was fêted through the streets of Dublin, received a commission in the army, and was knighted the following day by the Duke of Rutland, Lord Lieutenant. And Richard Crosbie? All Crosbie had to show for the day's endeavours was a bill for the £400 he had spent on preparations. Despite several more attempts, he never did succeed in crossing the Irish Sea in a balloon.

Irish stamp, issued 1985,
first flight by an Irishman

When Waters Run Red

23 May 2005

In the course of trying to persuade Pharaoh to allow the Israelites free passage from the land of Egypt, one of Moses's ploys was to turn the Nile a brilliant shade of red. According to Exodus 7:20-21: 'Lifting up the rod, he struck the water of the river, and it was turned into blood: And the fishes died and the river corrupted, and the Egyptians could not drink the water of the river.'

Other waters have run red more recently. In 1819, for example, when the much-loved King Kamahameha of Hawaii was approaching death, his imminent demise was indicated several days in advance by the arrival of an ominous 'red tide' in Honolulu harbour. Even today, almost universally, red tides bode ill.

A red tide, as we know it here in Ireland, is a variety of plankton. These tiny, often microscopic organisms float on the surface of the water and are at the mercy of every wind and current that may come their way. Those that are animal in nature are called zooplankton; those that are plants are phytoplankton.

At certain times of the year, notably in spring and autumn, phytoplankton can become very abundant for short periods, an event that is called a bloom. Like land plants, phytoplankton require light and nutrients to live and thrive; when the sun is bright and the concentrations of nitrates and phosphates in the water are coincidentally high, a bloom occurs and the numbers of phytoplankton may increase many thousandfold in a very short interval of time.

When blooms occur in the open sea, they can be a positive benefit to fish life; the situation being similar to that of cattle let out to graze on a rich green pasture. But there are hidden dangers to this sudden cornucopia. As they evolved, some of the tiny organisms learned to fight back in a rather clever way against being seen by the denizens of the deep as a free, floating lunch. A few species produce chemicals that discourage fish from eating them, and in some cases these substances are also toxic to humans. Although we rarely eat enough plankton ourselves to become ill, the toxin can sometimes be concentrated in significant amounts in shellfish and other consumers of the plankton, and the poison may then be ingested in toxic amounts by the unsuspecting human gourmet.

While some of these less pleasant species of phytoplankton are transparent or neutral in colour, others have a distinctly red or brownish tinge that colours the water when they bloom. It is the latter, known as dinoflagellates, that are mainly responsible for the red tides that occur from time to time off the southwest coast of Ireland, the most common offenders being *Dinophysis acuta* and *Dinophysis acuminata,* both of which produce a toxin known as okadaic acid.

Nocturne – Red Tide (oil on canvas)
Anne McWilliams

The History of the Pythia Restored

24 May 2005

The weather forecasters of today are the inheritors of a long and honourable tradition, even if the niche they occupy in futurology is narrower than that enjoyed by many of their predecessors. Perhaps the most famous of these forecasters of old were the oracles of ancient Greece, and of these, *primus inter pares* was the Delphic Oracle at the Temple of Apollo on the slopes of Mount Parnassus.

For centuries there was an accepted wisdom as to the origins of the Oracle at Delphi. It was said that goats feeding on Parnassus developed convulsions when they approached a certain deep cleft on the side of the mountain. This occurred because of a vapour exuding from the orifice, a vapour which was found to have a similar effect on humans. It was only a small step to impute the intoxicated ravings of those affected to divine inspiration from Apollo – the god, *inter alia*, of prophecy. And so in due course, the Temple of Apollo was erected on the spot.

The staff of the Temple included a rota of ladies to perform the role of Pythia. The duty-Pythia would inhale the hallowed fumes and fall into a trance; her divine ramblings were then interpreted by those who wished to know something of the future. Unfortunately, quite unlike today's forecasts, the message was sometimes ambiguous and frequently misleading.

Now, the story of the goats and fumes was universally believed until a young classicist called Adolphe Oppé went to Delphi in 1899. Adolphe said he saw no sign of any cleft among the rocks, and could find no trace of any gases that might induce hysterics in a Pythia. History, he more or less declared, was bunk, and his very persuasive essay to this effect became the new orthodoxy on the matter for nearly all the twentieth century.

In the early 1990s, however, geologist Jelle de Boer shared a bottle of wine with archaeologist John Hale in Portugal. De Boer, who knew the classical story of the Delphic Oracle but was unaware of the *fin de siècle* debunk, mentioned in passing that ten years previously he had documented the fault-line that passed beneath the Temple of Apollo. Nonsense! said Hale. Everyone knew now that there was no such geological phenomenon at Delphi. By the end of the bottle, the pair had agreed to investigate together.

In 1996 they not only confirmed the presence of the 'Delphi fault' de Boer had known about, but also discovered that it intersected yet another fault, the 'Kernafault', directly below the spot where the Pythia used to sit. They recruited a chemist to analyse the local spring water, and he identified therein small traces of ethylene; a toxicologist then confirmed for de Boer and Hale that exposure to ethylene in specific quantities could explain all the idiosyncrasies exhibited by the Pythia of old.

Thus, history, debunked for a century, had been authoritatively reinstated.

Priestess of Delphi, 1891 (oil on canvas), **John Collier (1850–1934)** Art Gallery of South Australia, Adelaide, Australia/Gift of the Rt. Honourable, the Earl of Kintore 1893/The Bridgeman Art Library

The Island of Oahu

26 May 2005

A large proportion of the Big Island of Hawaii, the largest of the archipelago, is occupied by the volcano Mauna Loa. On its slopes is the Mauna Loa Observatory, which has been monitoring the carbon dioxide content of our atmosphere for almost half a century. But the State Capital of Hawaii, Honolulu, is on the smaller island of Oahu, and this latter island is also home to another institution of vital interest to mankind: the Pacific Tsunami Warning Center is on Ewa Beach.

Tsunami monitoring on Oahu dates back to 1949, when a local warning centre was established following an incident a few years previously in which 160 people lost their lives. More important for the Pacific region as a whole, however, was an earthquake which occurred 45 years ago this week, on 22 May 1960, near the city of Concepción in Chile. Its epicentre was offshore, a large part of the tremor's energy was transferred into the ocean, and a tsunami raced across the Pacific faster than a jumbo jet.

Like all tsunamis, the wave was hardly noticeable over the open ocean, but the Oahu centre duly warned the local population. Cautious people moved to high ground, but the curious headed for the harbour to see the tsunami for themselves; for 60 people, the wave which arrived 14 hours after the tremor off the coast of Chile was the last thing that they would ever see. It struck Hawaii with such force that 22-tonne boulders were wrenched from the sea wall and parking meters were bent horizontal to the ground. Eight hours later the same wave killed some 200 people in Japan. Tsunamis reverberated around the Pacific for several days thereafter, until 2,000 lives had finally been lost. In the aftermath of this 1960 tsunami, 24 countries around the Pacific decided to pool their resources in the Pacific Tsunami Warning System, headquartered on Oahu island. Many of the countries already had, and indeed still have, their own local warning systems, but the events of 1960 had made it clear to all that an earthquake anywhere in the Pacific regions puts everyone at risk.

The Tsunami Warning Center in Hawaii, directly or indirectly, continuously monitors dozens of seismographs and tide-level gauges throughout the entire Pacific region. When a tremor of sufficient magnitude occurs, and tide gauge evidence supports the likelihood of a tsunami, a 'tsunami warning' is issued for all coasts within three hours' range of the epicentre, and a 'tsunami watch' is initiated for locations between three and six hours' distance. It is a difficult decision. A false alarm clocks up over 40 million dollars in evacuation costs and increases the risk that people will ignore a future warning. But the enormous human cost of not being warned of the arrival of a big tsunami was tragically illustrated on another ocean by the events of 26 December and the succeeding days last year.

The Great Wave off Kanagawa, c.1831 (woodblock print), Katsushika Hokusai (1760–1849) *Wikimedia, Creative Commons*

A Colourful and Controversial Cloud

8 June 2005

There is a doubt as to when, and by whom, noctilucent clouds were first discovered. Most authorities put the date as 23 June 1885, and cite the observer as one Otto Jesse of the Berlin Astronomical Observatory. Others, however, say they were sighted two weeks earlier by another German, T.W. Backhouse, near the town of Kissingen on 8 June, which is 120 years today. It is also a matter of some controversy whether their discovery in 1885 was because nobody had ever noticed them before, or simply because they were not there to see.

The highest clouds normally visible in the sky are rarely more than eight kilometres above the ground. But noctilucent clouds occur in a very narrow zone about 80 km up, at the very coldest level of the atmosphere; they are also very, very rare. Their texture is such that they are not seen during the day, because the sun just shines right through them. They are visible only at twilight, when the sun is between six and 16 degrees below the horizon. In such circumstances, the clouds are still sunlit because of their great height, while any ground-based observers are shrouded in darkness.

Noctilucent clouds appear low in the northern sky and have a silvery white appearance, often with a bluish tinge. They can be distinguished from ordinary high clouds by the fact that they are not tinted by the usual red glow of twilight; they also stand out brightly against the afterglow, in contrast to the familiar high cirrus clouds which appear dark.

It may be that the previously unnoticed noctilucent cloud was first spotted in 1885 because the sky was being closely watched that year for spectacular sunsets associated with the recent eruption of Krakatoa in the East Indies. Others maintain, however, that noctilucent clouds are a latter-day phenomenon. Their formation depends on the presence of significant amounts of water vapour at high levels in the atmosphere. Water vapour at these heights is known to be a by-product of the breakdown of methane, and levels of methane in the atmosphere have been steadily increasing since the advent of the industrial era. The increasing abundance of methane may well be the reason why noctilucent clouds appear to be more common nowadays.

Noctilucent clouds are seen most frequently between the latitudes of 50 and 65 degrees north, and here in Ireland, as one might expect, they are reported more frequently in the north than in the south. They are a summer phenomenon, seen mainly in the months from June through August. Moreover, the frequency of noctilucent clouds has a year-to-year variation coinciding closely with the 11-year solar sunspot cycle, reaching a peak at that point in the cycle when solar activity is at a minimum. We are close to that point at present, so the chances of seeing noctilucent clouds are better than usual this year.

Noctilucent clouds © Daragh McDonough

To See Ourselves as Others See Us

14 June 2005

Giraldus Cambrensis, Gerald of Wales, was one of the most colourful and formidable clerics of his generation. He was born around 1146 in Pembrokeshire, a member of a prominent Norman family who participated in King Henry II's incursions into Ireland. Over the years Gerald refused several bishoprics, hoping at some point to be offered what he considered the greatest prize of all, the Primacy of Wales, but ultimately, he achieved no higher office than the Archdeaconate of Brecon. Gerald played a prominent part in his eventful times, however, and visited Ireland on a number of occasions, outlining his views on our country in his book, *Topographia Hiberniae*.

Now, Gerald did not mince his words about the Irish whom, clearly, he disliked. 'They are a wild and inhospitable people, and they live like beasts,' he wrote. 'Moreover, above all other peoples they always practise treachery; when they give their word to anyone, they do not keep it.' And of those involved in agriculture, he says: 'They use the fields generally as pasture, but pasture in poor condition. Little is cultivated and even less is sown. And how few kinds of fruit-bearing trees are to be found here! The nature of the soil is not to be blamed but rather the want of industry on the part of the cultivator; he is too lazy to plant foreign types of trees that would grow well here.'

When it comes to the Irish weather, however, Gerald gives credit where it is due: 'This is the most temperate of all countries,' he writes. 'Summer does not here drive you to take shade from its burning heat; nor does the cold of winter send you rushing to the fire. You will seldom see snow here, and even then it lasts only for a short time. The air is so healthy that there is no disease-bearing cloud, nor pestilential vapour or corrupting breeze.'

But our climate, too, has its drawbacks: 'For this country more than others suffers from storms of wind and rain. What is born and comes forth in the spring, and is nourished in the summer and advanced, can scarcely be reaped in the harvest because of the unceasing rain.' He goes on to note 'such an ever-present overhanging of the clouds and fog, that you will scarcely see, even in summer, three consecutive days of really fine weather'.

And then, of course, the wind: 'A northwest wind, along with the west wind to its south, prevails here, and is more frequent and violent than any other. It bends in the opposite direction, or uproots, nearly all the trees in the west that are in elevated places.'

But Gerald concludes grudgingly that 'there is no disturbance of the air or inclemency of the weather that should inconvenience those who are in good health and spirits, or distress those that may suffer from disorders of the nervous kind.'

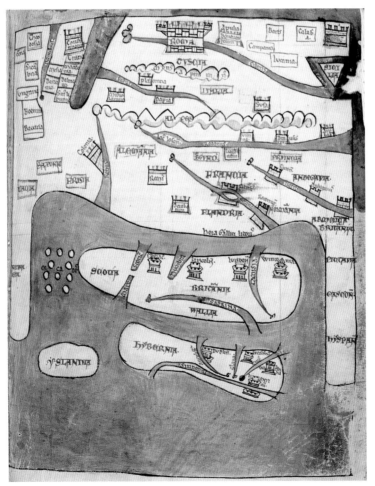

Map of Europe showing Ireland and England, Topographia Hiberniae, *National Library, Dublin*

The Elements against the Emperor

18 June 2005

'A few drops of water,' wrote Victor Hugo half a century after the event, 'a mere unseasonable cloud crossing the sky, sufficed for the overthrow of an entire world.'

In 1814, the Emperor Napoleon had been forced to abdicate. In March the following year, however, he escaped from Elba where he was in exile, and re-entered Paris to a rapturous welcome. By 15 June he was crossing into Belgium at the head of the Armée du Nord to fend off invasion by General von Blücher and the Duke of Wellington; on the 16th he took on von Blücher's Prussian troops at Ligny, and he won. Then he set off in pursuit of the Anglo-Dutch contingent under Wellington, who had retreated to a safe position near the little town of Waterloo, just south of Brussels.

Meanwhile, however, on 17 June, a small but very active depression moved eastwards along the English Channel. It was remarkable for its very heavy falls of thundery rain, which in the vicinity of Brussels continued until breakfast-time the following morning and turned the fields of Belgium into quagmire.

Now, Napoleon was the master of the quick manoeuvre. His success as a general rested largely on his being able to deal a crushing blow to the weakest spot when it was least expected. He would use his artillery as one might aim a pistol, continually searching for the point where maximum advantage might be gained, and reacting to the ebb and flow of fortune at different places on the battlefield. For these tactics dry ground and a firm footing were essential; both were denied to him at Waterloo.

The French attack on Wellington had been planned for 8am on the morning of this day, 18 June, 190 years ago. But with the fields a sea of mud after the heavy rain, it was apparent that the French artillery and cavalry would be unable to advance across the fields in any sort of order. Having surveyed the dismal scene, the Emperor postponed attack in the hope that the sun might come out and dry the soil. But the sun did not appear, and the ground did not dry up; it was almost noon before Napoleon accepted the inevitable, and ordered the attack.

Until mid-afternoon the battle went in favour of the French. But the four-hour delay turned out to be decisive; it had allowed von Blücher the extra time he needed to regroup from his defeat, and when the Prussian reinforcements arrived in Waterloo at 4pm they turned the tide of battle. 'It was a damned nice thing,' the Duke of Wellington was heard to say afterwards, 'the nearest run thing you ever saw in your life.' But it ended in defeat for the Emperor Napoleon, and he abdicated for the final time a few days later to spend the remaining six years of his life on the lonely island of St. Helena in the South Atlantic.

Wellington at Waterloo, 1892 (oil on canvas), **Ernest Crofts (1847–1911),** Private Collection Photo © Bonhams, London, UK/The Bridgeman Art Library

The Remains of the Day

20 June 2005

You remember, don't you, that idyllic evening in *The Wind in the Willows* on which Mole waits for Water Rat to bring the latest news concerning the disappearance of young Portly Otter? 'Though it was past ten o'clock at night, the sky still clung to and retained some lingering skirts of light from the departed day; and the sullen heats of the torrid afternoon broke up and rolled away at the dispersing touch of the cool fingers of the short midsummer night. Mole lay stretched on the river bank, still panting from the stress of the fierce day that had been cloudless from dawn to late sunset, and waited for his friend's return.'

We have been able to empathise with Mole's experience in recent days. At our latitude the length of twilight varies through the year, depending on the angle made by the path of the setting sun with the horizon. At a large angle of incidence, such as occurs around the equinoxes, the sun shoots straight down behind the horizon with no nonsense, and twilight lasts only for an hour or so. But at this time of year, near the summer solstice, the path of the setting sun is at a relatively shallow angle to the horizon, and it takes considerably longer for darkness to set in.

Normally the term twilight is restricted to the evening light, the pleasant afterglow of the departing day; we usually call the morning twilight 'dawn'. The former begins at sunset, which strictly speaking, occurs the instant the upper edge or 'limb' of the solar disc appears to coincide with the horizon. Allowing for the effects of refraction – the bending of the rays of light from the sun by the atmosphere – sunset occurs when the sun's centre is geometrically slightly less than one degree below the horizon.

The end of twilight, however, is less clear-cut. So-called 'civil twilight', for example, on which 'lighting up time' is based, ends when the centre of the solar disc is six degrees below the horizon, but 'nautical twilight', for many purposes a more useful definition, ends when the sun's centre is 12 degrees below. By this time it is, for all practical purposes, completely dark; the constellations can be distinguished overhead, and a distant horizon is no longer visible, except by moonlight.

At this time, around the summer solstice, nautical twilight lingers for two hours or more at the latitude of Cork. If you proceed northwards from there, however, you find twilight lengthening even further, by about one extra minute for every mile travelled, until at Belfast, nautical twilight lasts throughout the night. And, of course, if you were to continue northwards and cross the Arctic Circle, you would find yourself in the proverbial 'land of the midnight sun' where there is no darkness, no twilight of any kind, and where, when skies are cloudless, the sun is visible throughout the 24-hour day.

Landscape at Dusk, 1885 (oil on canvas), **Vincent Van Gogh** (1853–90)
Madrid, Museo Thyssen-Bornemisza © 2012 Museo Thyssen-Bornemisza Madrid

Midsummer Measures

23 June 2005

Some like to celebrate midsummer with a gay abandon, frolicking around neolithic monuments in their cool, diaphanous *déshabillé*. If you are one such, then this year you are too late; these celebrations took place at the summer solstice, which occurred two days ago on 21 June.

Meteorologists, on the other hand, approach midsummer from a different angle; noting that the three warmest months of the year in the northern hemisphere are June, July and August. They reckon that midsummer should fall about the middle of this period, on or around 15 July, which to add to the confusion, turns out to be St. Swithin's Day as well.

By popular tradition going back to pagan times, however, Midsummer's Day is 24 June, the feast of John the Baptist, and today, St. John's Eve, is noteworthy for the wealth of superstition that surrounds it. Another John, John Aubrey, was an expert on such matters.

Aubrey, who lived from 1626 to 1697, is best remembered for his whimsical biographies of Milton, Shakespeare and other well-known people of that time. Of Shakespeare, for example, he wrote: 'His father was a butcher, and I have been told it heretofore by some of the neighbours that when he was a boy he exercised his father's trade, and when he killed a calf he would do it in high style and make a speech.'

But Aubrey also knew about contemporary folklore. He notes that 'Midsummer Eve is called the Witches' Night; and still in many places on St. John's Eve they make fires upon the hills', a tradition common to many cultures throughout Europe. The date, too, like many others, was an important one in the calendar of wooing. Aubrey had this advice, for example, for young maidens, advice that for all we know may well be efficacious still: 'At midnight on Midsummer Eve walk several times around a church, clockwise, scattering hempseed and saying:

> *Hempseed I sow, hempseed I mow,*
> *Let him that is my true love come after me and show.*

Then look over your left shoulder and you will see, following behind you, the form of your predestined lover.'

Then girls whose *affaires de coeur* were rather more advanced could discover the state of their lovers' affections by observing the behaviour of a sprig of orpine, known colloquially as Midsummer Man. The plant was loosely clamped in clay, and the romance was fated to endure if it leaned over to the right, but doomed to end within the year if the plant was noticed listing to the left.

Young men, too, could avail of horticultural assistance. On Midsummer's Eve – one suspects with intentions that were sometimes less than honourable – they could become invisible by plucking fernseed, but for the ploy to succeed they had to do so on the stroke of midnight, and without making any contact with the plant itself. Not, alas, an easy task!

Midsummer Eve, c.1908 (watercolour on paper), **Edward Robert Hughes (1851–1914)** Private Collection/ Photo © The Maas Gallery, London/ The Bridgeman Art Library

The M'Naghten Rules, OK?

24 June 2005

Daniel M'Naghten, although he had no wish to be, was doubly famous. A simple Scottish woodsman, Mr. M'Naghten believed himself the victim of an international conspiracy in which the Pope and the Prime Minister, Sir Robert Peel, were both involved. In February 1843, he stalked Peel for several days, and when he saw a figure he believed to be the Prime Minister approaching Downing Street, he fired a single shot into the latter's back. But in a classic case of mistaken identity, it turned out that, instead, he had killed the PM's private secretary, Edward Drummond.

M'Naghten's second claim to fame came when, in due course, he was tried and found 'not guilty by reason of insanity'. The verdict caused considerable disquiet; Queen Victoria was not amused, and the House of Lords was strongly disapproving. The House of Lords appointed a committee of 15 judges to define the law on insanity, and the result was a set of principles which have ever since been known as the M'Naghten Rules. In essence, they lay down that to be judged insane a defendant must have been so mentally disturbed that he knew neither the 'nature or quality' of his act, or was incapable of realising that what he did was wrong.

Fine legal points like these are far above the heads of simple weatherfolk, but from time to time we do become entangled in the law; we engage in what we call forensic meteorology. In one celebrated case in Canada, for example, the body of a murder victim had not been found for some considerable time, and the prime suspect had strong alibis for much of the intervening period. Careful reconstruction of the exact temperature pattern in the two days prior to the discovery of the body, however, made it possible to calculate the precise rate of cooling of the body, and to pin-point the time of death to within an hour or two, to a time for which the suspect had no alibi.

In another case, the body of a young woman was found on a dry, bright evening, lying, naturally enough, on ground that was completely dry. But an astute police officer noted that the inside of a rain hat, folded in her handbag, happened to be wet. From this it was inferred that the woman must have been killed shortly after a heavy shower of rain.

Old Man in Sorrow (On the Threshold of Eternity) 1890 (oil on canvas), **Vincent Van Gogh** (1853–90)/Rijksmuseum Kröller-Müller, Otterlo, The Netherlands/The Bridgeman Art Library

Enter a meteorologist. Given the approximate time of death, he was able to use satellite pictures and rainfall records to identify places where showers had occurred; since there were few showers that day, the police were able to focus their enquiries on just one or two likely areas, and solved the case.

But what happened to that poor young man M'Naghten? Despite, or perhaps because of, the verdict at his trial, Daniel M'Naghten was forcibly institutionalised for the remainder of his life. He died in Broadmoor around 1865.

Choose Your God of Thunder

29 June 2005

'*Si Dieu n'existait pas,*' declared Voltaire, '*il faudrait l'inventer.*' If God did not exist, it would be necessary to invent him. And so we did in ancient times. In the absence of a more scientific explanation for familiar meteorological phenomena, our ancestors assigned the relevant responsibility to some plausible deity. Thunder and lightning was a prime portfolio.

Strangely, perhaps, the thunder gods were rarely evil or unfriendly. Their frequent and spectacular visits to their earthly domains were welcomed, and the gods themselves were seen as a benign influence on the affairs of men. This may have been, perhaps, because in many climates a thunderstorm often heralded the end of a long drought, and the heavy rain obligingly provided by the passing deity softened the baked earth, giving the promise of a fruitful harvest in due course.

The American Indians, or Native Americans as we like to call them now, had a picturesque imagination in these matters. The Algonquins, for example, thought of lightning as a great serpent periodically vomited out by Manitou, the Creator. They were inspired, no doubt, by lightning's quick spring and sharp recoil, and by the sinuosity and sheer unpredictability of its rapid movement. The Pawnees, on the other hand, believed that lightning was produced by the magical thunderbird, its vivid plumage and the beating of its wings as it dived from the dark clouds providing, respectively, the flash of lightning and the peal of thunder. The rainbow was seen as the thunderbird's dying breath, as it expired under the powerful influence of the sacred sun.

In the real India, however, the god of thunder in ancient times was Indra, who was transported noisily across the sky in a golden carriage drawn by two thousand horses. The epic Sanskrit poem the *Mahabharata* a describes how he inaugurates the summer monsoon: 'Indra covers the entire firmament with masses of blue clouds, and those clouds luminous with lightning and incessantly roaring against each other in the welkin, pour abundant water; with the falling torrents, the deep roar of the clouds, the flashes of lightning and the violence of the winds, the sky looks as if it is dancing in madness.'

The Greeks and Romans shared a god of thunder, albeit by a different name. To the Greeks he was Zeus, depicted on a throne with thunderbolt in hand, ready to strike his enemies, while the Romans knew him by the name of Jupiter. In Norse mythology, on the other hand, Wotan was in charge of thunder, and farther south, in what we now know as Germany, the relevant Teutonic god was Thor, who wielded a mighty hammer with which he split the clouds. Those dark Teutonic thunderclouds comprised a mixture of water and an inflammable vapour called 'vafermist'; when the cloud was split, the two were separated, the former falling as rain and the latter catching fire and descending earthwards as lightning.

*Statue of Zeus, after Phidias
at the State Hermitage Museum*
George Shuklin, *Wikipedia Commons*

What Was the Weather in Wonderland?

4 July 2005

'I believe the beginning of Alice was told one summer afternoon when the sun was so burning hot that we had landed in the meadows down the river, deserting the boat to take refuge in the only bit of shade to be found, which was under a new-made hay-rick. Here, from all three of us, came the old petition of "Tell us a story," and so began the ever-delightful tale.' Thus did the eponymous Alice Liddell remember *Alice's Adventures in Wonderland* in the autumn of her life some 80 years ago.

The famous fantasy was first related on a boating trip on the River Isis not too far from Oxford. The party was led by the Rev. Charles Lutwidge Dodgson, a mathematician at the university who later became much better known to posterity by his *nom de plume* of Lewis Carroll. The other participants were Alice Liddell and her sisters, Edith and Lorina. They rowed to Godstow and back, enjoying, as Alice said, a warm sunny afternoon upon the river.

Dodgson was born in 1832, and the great success of his fantastic stories has been attributed to the fact that, unlike most material for children at the time, they had no obvious moral to them and did not claim to teach anything. He was a keen amateur photographer, with a particular interest – a pastime, it must be said, which would be looked at nowadays askance – in photographing young girls, whose friendship, we are told, he valued very highly.

But *Alice*, too, is not without its share of controversy. Dodgson in his diary confirms Alice's recollection of a warm sunny afternoon, and what is more, the diary tells us when it was; the relevant entry is that for 4 July 1862, 143 years ago today. But then literary historians with little else to do looked up the Oxford rainfall records, and discovered that there was a significant amount of rainfall in the 12 hours prior to 2am on 5 July. They concluded that the afternoon of 4 July must have been dull and rather wet, and that the diary entry must be spurious or that memories were playing tricks.

Since conventional weather maps for the early 1860s do not exist, modern meteorologists seeking to resolve this important controversy had to rely on contemporary weather reports from British harbours published in *The Times*.

Using these as one might use modern weather observations, they reconstructed weather maps for the period in question. This analysis showed that an active front had passed the Oxford area in the early morning of 4 July, and another moved in from the west late that evening to give the rain already noted from the rainfall records. In between, however, in the early afternoon of 4 July, a weak ridge of high pressure would have allowed for fine conditions, a welcome vindication of the evidence provided to posterity by the main protagonists.

The Three Sisters of Dean Liddell (oil on canvas), **Sir William Blake Richmond (1842–1921)**; Private Collection; (figure on the left is Alice; 2nd daughter of Henry George (1811–98) – later Mrs Reginald Hargreaves; The Bridgeman Art Library

Whymper's Apparition

14 July 2005

'A mighty arch appeared, rising high into the sky. Pale, colourless and noiseless, but perfectly sharp and defined, except where it was lost in cloud, this unearthly apparition seemed like a vision from another world, and almost appalled we watched with amazement the gradual development of two vast crosses, one on either side. It was a fearful and wonderful sight in the circumstances, unique in my experience, and impressive beyond description.'

'Whymper's apparition', one of the classic stories in mountaineering history, appeared on the evening of a tragic day for Edward Whymper. As a 20-year-old artist in 1860, Whymper had been commissioned by a fellow Englishman to paint Alpine scenes, and took to climbing mountains. By 1865, after several unsuccessful attempts to climb the southwestern face of the Matterhorn, he became convinced that the mountain could be conquered from its eastern flank. He was right, and he and six companions became the first persons successfully to climb the Matterhorn 140 years ago today, on 14 July 1865.

Triumph turned to tragedy on the descent. One member of the party lost his footing, and as he fell he dragged three of his companions with him. Only the breaking of a rope saved Whymper and the two remaining guides from the same fate. 'For a few seconds we saw our unfortunate companions sliding downwards on their backs, and spreading out their hands, endeavouring to save themselves. They disappeared one by one, and fell from precipice to precipice on to the glacier below, a distance of 4,000 feet.' It was in the hours subsequent to this accident, as the shocked survivors continued down the mountainside, that they saw the apparition – and meteorologists in the intervening years have been wondering what it was.

The arch, some say, is likely to have been a fogbow, a phenomenon similar to a rainbow except that the light is reflected from tiny fog droplets rather than drops of rain. The very small reflecting droplets produce a bow that is white, or colourless.

Moreover, if a thin cloud of ice crystals is present in the sky, and if, by virtue of their being a very special shape, the ice crystals are orientated all in the same direction, they act like millions of tiny mirrors to reflect the sun's rays in a number of specific patterns. One such is a parhelic circle, a horizontal line of light passing through the sun, but stretching, if atmospheric conditions are exactly right, around the full 360 degrees parallel to the horizon. It has been suggested that the two crosses of Whymper's apparition may have been the apparent intersection of portions of a parhelic circle and a fogbow.

In any event, Whymper survived his ordeal to climb more mountains, but the tragedy haunted him throughout his life. He became solitary, irascible and morose, and much given to heavy drinking. He died, aged 71, in 1911 at Chamonix in France.

Whymper's Apparition (engraving) from Scrambles Across The Alps in 1860–69, **Edward Whymper**

A Calculated Sense of Direction

22 July 2005

A compass needle, as we know, only very rarely points exactly north. Both of the Earth's magnetic poles lie at present about 15 degrees of latitude from their respective geographic counterparts, and as a result there is nearly always a slight difference between what is called true (or geographic) north and magnetic north (the direction to which a compass needle points). The angle between the two is called by scientists the 'declination', and by mariners the 'compass variation'.

The magnetic declination is not constant; it differs from place to place, and at any particular spot it changes gradually over the years. At Valentia Observatory in County Kerry, for example, the variation has steadily decreased from 21 degrees in 1900 to about 7 degrees today, and the variation decreases by about 2 degrees as one moves eastwards across the country from Galway towards Dublin. The variation in all these cases is westerly; magnetic north lies to the west of true north, and the correction must be subtracted from the compass reading to get a true bearing.

Lines drawn on a map connecting places with the same magnetic declination are called isogonics, and they run crookedly in a more or less north-south direction. Of particular interest is the isogonic line of zero declination, connecting those places in the world where a compass reads exactly right. It almost bisects both North and South America, running from Hudson Bay through the Great Lakes, cutting the island of Cuba into two, before heading down through western Brazil to Buenos Aires. At points to the east of this line the declination is to the west of geographic north, while all points to the west of it share an easterly variation.

The changes in the Earth's magnetic field in these parts are monitored continuously at three geophysical observatories: Valentia Observatory, Hartland Point in Devon and Eskdalemuir Observatory outside Edinburgh. Every so often, however, the finer detail has to be filled in by means of a 'magnetic survey'. Here in Ireland this involves a small team of observers, equipped with the appropriate instruments, travelling the country every five years or so and carrying out precise measurements of the declination and other magnetic parameters at 14 so-called 'repeat stations' scattered around the country. These repeat station sites are carefully chosen so that they can be used again and again over many decades, being located, for example, in conservation areas, on publicly owned property or on lands that are otherwise unlikely to be developed.

Using the data from the magnetic surveys, the maps showing the Irish isogonic lines are regularly updated, so that at any given time accurate information is available to anyone who needs it about the extent to which a compass will deviate from true north anywhere in the country.

> *And thus do we of wisdom and of reach,*
> *With windlasses and with assays of bias*
> *By indirections find directions out.*

Aurora Borealis
NASA

When Will the Compass Do a Sudden Flip?

23 July 2005

In the days of the old sailing vessels, it was firmly believed that both garlic and onions affected the accuracy of the magnetic compass. For this reason, neither was allowed aboard a ship, and the mariners of old were deprived of the benefit of either form of seasoning. But a compass needle, as we noted yesterday, will rarely point exactly north anyway. The difference between true (or geographic) north and magnetic north (the direction to which a compass needle points) is called 'declination' or 'compass variation', and changes both with time and from place to place around the world.

Columbus was somewhat taken aback by this phenomenon of declination on his first voyage towards the New World, but he wisely kept his worries to himself; he was afraid that if his crew became aware of this strange occurrence, they might become terrified and insist on turning back. But once the concept became familiar, later mariners began to notice that the declination seemed to change more or less uniformly as one moved from east to west or vice versa. Moreover, it could be easily measured by taking a bearing on the pole star and comparing this to that given by the compass. So it struck them that here was a convenient way of establishing one's longitude: if you knew the rate at which the declination changed as you moved westwards, all you had to do was compare the declination at your place of observation with that at places whose longitude had already been determined.

But a wider experience taught them that it was not as simple as it seemed. The lines of equal declination do not always run north–south, and even where they do, declination could not be measured accurately enough at sea to make the method a viable one for estimating longitude.

Geological evidence, however, suggests that the Earth's magnetic field has undergone even more dramatic changes over the millennia. Every 500,000 years or so, it seems, the system 'flips', and, over a relatively short period – short in geological time, at any rate – the magnetic field undergoes complete reversal; the north magnetic pole becomes the south, and vice versa.

The last time this happened was about three-quarters of a million years ago, so the inference is that a 'flip' is overdue. Some scientists have been bold enough to predict that it will occur about 2,000 years from now, and have speculated on the interesting navigational problems likely to be encountered by those fish, birds and other animals that use the Earth's magnetic field to get their bearings. Others, however, suggest that even though such a change might be sudden on a geologic timescale, it would be gradual – say over 1,000 years or so – in terms of animal and human life. Any organisms still around in AD 4000 will have had ample time to become acclimatised.

Computer-generated diagram showing the process of magnetic reversal, NASA

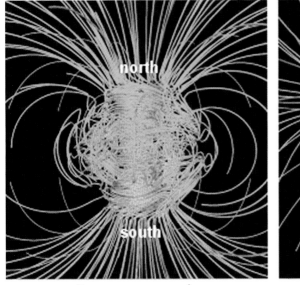 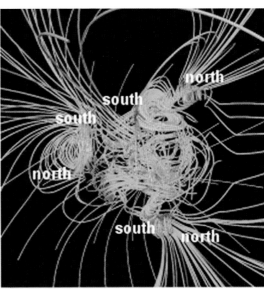

Between reversals   During a reversal

Academic Sleuths Pursue Van Gogh

27 July 2005

Vincent Van Gogh spent most of 1889 in the mental hospital at Saint-Rémy, near Arles in the south of France. He was allowed considerable latitude in this institution, and although subject to intermittent periods of mental instability, he produced 150 paintings during his time there. In the asylum's walled gardens he painted irises, lilacs and ivy-covered trees, and when allowed to venture farther afield, he portrayed the wheat fields, olive groves and cypress trees of the surrounding countryside.

Vincent corresponded frequently and regularly with his younger brother Theo in Paris, and it is from this correspondence that many of his paintings have been accurately dated. Sometimes, however, as in the case of *Evening Landscape with Rising Moon,* there is insufficient information in the letters.

Moonrise, as it is sometimes called, shows a field with haystacks and a full moon rising over distant hills, and Dr. Donald Olsen of the Texas State University saw that the position of the moon could be used to pinpoint the precise time of execution of the painting. He visited Saint-Rémy, identified from the painting itself the artist's exact vantage-point, and then calculated when a rising full moon would have appeared above the landscape where Van Gogh portrayed it. The exercise produced two dates: 16 May and 13 July. But mid-May is too early in the year for haystacks, so Olsen concluded that the scene was portrayed as it would have appeared at 9.08pm, local time, on 13 July 1889.

Another academic, this time a Cambridge mathematician called John Barrow, has suggested that another of Van Gogh's Saint-Rémy paintings, *The Starry Night,* may have an interesting connection with Birr Castle. The picture portrays the local landscape in semi-darkness, but the work is dominated by a large spiral pattern in the sky whose significance has puzzled art historians for decades.

Professor Barrow, however, has pointed out that the spiral pattern exactly resembles a sketch of the M51 galaxy executed by the third Earl of Rosse. Rosse produced many such drawings to illustrate his discoveries with the 72-inch reflector telescope at Birr, which was for many years the largest in the world. Barrow points out that the Earl's sketch of M51 was included in a contemporary textbook called *Popular*

The Starry Night, 1889 (oill on canvas), **Vincent Van Gogh** (1853–90)
The Museum of Modern Art, New York/The Bridgeman Art Library

Astronomy by Camille Flammarion of the Paris Observatory, a work that was a French bestseller in its day; Van Gogh might well have had access to a copy, and used the Earl of Rosse's sketch as the basis for *The Starry Night*.

In May 1890, the 37-year-old Van Gogh moved to Auvers-sur-Oise, near Paris, to be closer to his brother, but his mental health did not improve. Two months later, on 27 July, 115 years ago today, he walked to a nearby wheat field and shot himself in the chest. He survived the shot, but died two days later with Theo at his side.

Forty Shades of Blue

28 July 2005

Why make so much of fragmentary blue
In here and there a bird, or butterfly,
Or flower, or wearing-stone, or open eye,
When heaven presents in sheets the solid hue?

Robert Frost's question, one has to say, was based on a false premise. The sky, in fact, is rarely, if ever, a solid blue, but rather a wide variety of different shades. Indeed at various times it can be almost any colour you care to mention; it can be, like Shelley's autumn, 'yellow, and black, and pale, and hectic red', depending on the circumstances and the time of day.

To understand why, we must recall why the daytime sky tends to be blue in the first place. Light coming from the sun is white light, a mixture of all the colours of the spectrum. But light, as it travels through the atmosphere, is subject to a process known as scattering; it is obstructed by any tiny particles in its way, and even by the molecules of the air itself, and deflected away from its original path.

The effectiveness of this scattering process depends both on the colour of the light and the size of the scattering particles. When the atmosphere is very clean, the tiny molecules of air scatter only the very short wavelengths of blue and violet light; the longer wavelengths, the red and orange parts of the solar spectrum, and indeed all the other colours, surge straight through the atmosphere, virtually unaffected. So when you look upwards at the sky, away from the sun, what you see is the blue portion of sunlight that had originally been headed in an entirely different direction, but which has been scattered towards you by the atmosphere.

The blueness of the sky differs from place to place. The skies over the Greek islands, for example, are a deep, deep blue. And those over Ireland on a fresh showery day are an even richer shade of the same colour. But skies over continental Europe are paler by comparison, a study in pastels quite anaemic to our Irish eyes. Why the variation?

It depends to a large extent on the purity of the air. The air over Europe contains a much greater concentration of dust particles and other impurities arising from industrial and other sources than does our Atlantic air. These particles are many times larger than the molecules of the air itself, and are capable of scattering, not just the blue portion of the incoming light, but many of the other constituent colours of sunlight as well. As a result, the mixture of scattered light that reaches our eyes, while predominantly blue, contains also a mixture of many other colours, making for a tendency towards white. For this reason, the Continental sky is a generally much paler shade of blue than that which we are accustomed to at home.

The Great Fish Market, 1603 (oil on oak panel), Jan Brueghel (1568–1625)
From the Mannheim Gallery © bpk/Bayerische Staatsgemäldesammlungen

The Delights of a Red Evening Sky

29 July 2005

Perhaps the most evocative pen-picture ever of a red sunset is that drawn by Henry Wadsworth Longfellow in 'The Song of Hiawatha', when the crimson sky over Gitche Gumee, Big-Sea-Water, is pointed out to the young warrior by an old Indian woman called Nokomis:

> *Fiercely the red sun descending,*
> *Burned his way along the heavens,*
> *Set the sky on fire behind him,*
> *As war-parties, when retreating,*
> *Burn the prairies on their war-trail.*

These optical pyrotechnics are a product of the same process of scattering which gives us our blue skies, and which we discussed yesterday in *Weather Eye*. This time, however, the process works, as it were, in reverse.

White sunlight is a mixture of all the colours of the spectrum. As it travels through the Earth's atmosphere, it is obstructed, or scattered, by any tiny particles in its path, and even by the molecules of the air itself. In this way the atmosphere acts as a kind of filter which affects some of the constituent colours of the sunlight more than others.

Now, in the middle of the day, when the sun is high in the sky and shining almost vertically downwards, the path of the light through the atmosphere is relatively short. In this situation only a little light in the very shortest wavelengths of blue and violet is filtered out, and the noonday sun appears to be as near white as makes no difference. But when we look towards the evening sun sinking below the horizon, the light has reached us after passing very obliquely through the atmosphere; it has had a much longer journey through the air than when the sun was directly overhead. This longer path allows for more filtering, so by the time the sunlight reaches us, its 'bluer' constituents – the violet, blue and green light – have been almost totally extracted; only the red and yellow wavelengths are left to decorate the twilight sky.

The effectiveness of the atmospheric filter also depends on the size of the scattering particles. Filtering is at a minimum when the air is clean and dry; the setting sun is bright yellow and the adjacent sky shows various shades of yellow and orange. But a polluted atmosphere removes all wavelengths of light except red; the sun appears a reddy-orange, and the sky a deep, dull red. On a day when pollution is particularly heavy, the sun may be a dull red disc that fades away even before it reaches the horizon.

A moisture-laden atmosphere is also very efficient at the filtering process, and provides some of our most lurid sunsets. Only if the evening sky is a pale and delicate shade of yellowish pink – indicating a clean, dry atmosphere – can we depend to any extent on the old adage that 'a red sky at night is the shepherd's delight'.

Harvest Home, Sunset 1856 (oil on canvas), John Linnell (1792–1882)
© Tate Gallery

A Subcontinent Given to Extremes

30 July 2005

The Indian monsoon system resembles our own sea breeze phenomenon re-enacted on a grand scale. As the heat of the summer sun intensifies, the air over the vast Asian landscape expands and becomes lighter, causing a low-pressure area to develop over the middle of the continent in June or early July. Then, with the anti-clockwise motion around this low, warm moist air from the Indian Ocean is drawn in over India from the southwest. The warm humid air is forced to rise as it crosses the gently sloping Plateau of the Deccan towards the Himalayan Mountains; clouds form, and ultimately open to disgorge torrential rains.

The summer monsoon rejuvenates a dying landscape. Through each blistering spring, the arid soil has been baked lifeless by burning sun and desiccating winds, and inhabitants of the subcontinent move about their business at a weary, listless pace. Then, just when the heat seems insupportable, the rains descend in torrents on a grateful land. They are celebrated almost as divine deliverance; children dance ecstatically in the heavy downpour, catching the precious drops of liquid in their open hands as the stifling heat is broken and the earth blooms forth in fresh and green profusion.

But the monsoon regime is characterised by a very high degree of variability. Now and then the rains are delayed or weaker than usual, so that livestock suffer, agricultural production falls, and great hardships are visited on large sections of the local population; sometimes the monsoon fails completely, and if failures are repeated over several seasons the results are catastrophic. At other times, as at present, the monsoon rains may be exceptionally heavy, and the superabundant waters, flowing over a land baked as hard as concrete by the early summer sun, sweep away and drown hundreds of people in their muddy tides. Weather extremes might be said to be the norm in India.

The summer monsoon rainfall averaged over the whole of India has been more or less stable for 120 years since it first was measured, and shows little signs of systematic change. It has been noted, however, that in the state of Gujarat, in the vicinity of the Rann of Kutch, and also down the west coast of the subcontinent – which includes Mumbai – there has been a trend in recent decades for an increased frequency of heavy falls of summer monsoon rain. While this week's events cannot be immediately put down to global warming, they are at least consistent with this trend.

The monsoon rains normally continue intermittently until late September, delivering in the few months of their duration about 90 per cent of the subcontinent's annual rainfall. As the cold season re-approaches, however, the continental anticyclone over Siberia reasserts itself; the air-flow once again reverses direction, bringing back the dry northeasterly winds of the winter monsoon. India dries out, and prepares for the droughts that will inevitably affect many parts the following spring.

Indian satellite image showing monsoon clouds over the subcontinent
India Meteorological Department

Dangers Posed by Leonardo's Downburst

2 August 2005

The next time you find yourself waiting for someone in the Royal Library at Windsor Castle, cast your eye over the series of 11 drawings held there known collectively as *A Deluge*, executed by Leonardo da Vinci around 1515. Some meteorologists are convinced that one of these, the one known uncharismatically as Drawing No.12380, is an accurate representation of the phenomenon we call a microburst.

A microburst is a vicious side effect of a thunderstorm: a sudden, highly localised downward gush of air which hits the ground at speed and bursts out horizontally in all directions around the point of impact, rather like the stream of water from a tap when it strikes the bottom of the kitchen sink. As Leonardo himself put it, having allegedly deduced the *modus operandi* of a thunderstorm: 'The winds descend from above to below at various angles, and striking earth or water, set up lateral motions along various lines.'

A full-blown microburst is a comparatively rare event in western Europe, but they are common enough in the United States. An aircraft that flies into a microburst when landing first encounters an unexpected headwind which increases lift. Seconds later comes the downdraught, whose effect on the behaviour of the aircraft is exacerbated if the pilot has already compensated for the upward thrust just recently encountered; and finally a tail-wind results in a sharp drop in airspeed, and an even more rapid loss of height.

This vicious sequence of sudden, unexpected wind-shifts can be lethal, as indeed it was 20 years ago today on 2 August 1985, for Delta Airlines Flight DL 191 from Fort Lauderdale to Dallas. The TriStar aircraft encountered a microburst while landing around 6pm; a mile or so short of the runway it crashed onto a highway, collided with two water tanks, and then broke up in flames. One hundred and thirty-four people lost their lives.

Today's aircraft, although safer and more sophisticated in many other ways, are potentially more vulnerable to turbulence of this kind than their older counterparts. The typical propeller-driven aircraft of the 1950s landed at about 100 mph, and its reciprocating engine responded to the controls in about two seconds. Modern jets, however, land at about 150 mph, and their engines may take up to seven seconds to respond fully to pilot input. Looked at another way, during take-off and landing, a 1950s' aircraft would have flown about 100 yards before the engines responded; the corresponding distance for today's jets is well over a quarter of a mile. Such differences in the response time can be crucial when coping with a microburst.

Luckily, downdrafts associated with even the worst of Irish thunderstorms are not normally sufficiently severe to merit the term microburst. And in any event, modern Doppler radars can 'see' the wind, and allow microbursts to be identified for what they are and accurately observed, so that pilots can avoid the areas of danger.

A Deluge, c.1517–18 (pen & ink with wash on paper), **Leonardo da Vinci (1452–1519)**
The Royal Collection © 2011 Her Majesty Queen Elizabeth II/The Bridgeman Art Library

Testing Times for Job

13 August 2005

Zophar, Bildad and Eliphaz acquired an unenviable niche in biblical history as the proverbial comforters of the Patriarch Job.

They had journeyed from afar, you may recall, sometime in the evil days between the Deluge and the call of Abraham, and found poor Job in a very sorry state indeed. Some time previously a great storm had come down from the desert and swept away the house in which Job's children were assembled, crushing them to death; then robbers made off with all his camels, his asses and his oxen; and finally on Job himself there fell the terrible and awful scourge of leprosy. The visitors found the poor old man debilitated and alone, deserted, cursed and childless.

All this was in stark contrast to the cheerful Job they used to know and love. He had been rich and happy, had enjoyed life, and dutifully praised God who had blessed him with such comfort and contentment. Observing the great change, the visitors tactlessly suggested to Job that he must have sinned a great deal to have brought such calamities down upon his head.

The facts, of course, were very different. God, goaded a little by the devil, Satan, had showered all these nasty happenings on Job merely to try the latter's mettle. In due course, however, He severely rebuked the three misguided comforters – curtly dismissing them 'lest I deal with you after your folly' – but before finally calling a halt to the unfortunate adventure, He gave Job a long lecture on complacency. It included a *viva voce* on weather matters which would serve admirably as the final examination in any Institute of Meteorology: 'Hast thou entered into the store-houses of the snow; or hast thou beheld the treasures of the hail?' He asks Job: 'By what way is the light spread and heat divided on the Earth? Who gave a course to violent showers or a way for noisy thunder? Can any understand the spreadings of the clouds? Who is the father of the rain? And who begot the drops of the dew? And the frost from heaven – who hath gendered it? Canst thou lift up thy voice to the clouds, that an abundance of waters may cover thee? Canst thou send lightnings – and will they go? Dost thou know the balancings of the clouds?'

Job's patience must have been sorely tried, but he seems to have passed the test with flying colours. In any event, the Book of Job has a happy ending, as God more than restores the status quo: 'And the Lord blessed the latter end of Job more than the beginning, and gave him twice as much as he had had before. And Job lived after these things a hundred and forty years and he saw his children and his children's children unto the fourth generation and he died an old man, full of days.'

Still Life with Bible, 1885 (oil on canvas), **Vincent Van Gogh** (1853–90)
Van Gogh Museum, Amsterdam, The Netherlands/The Bridgeman Art Library

The Conventional Sign of the Zig-Zag Line

16 August 2005

Lewis Carroll poses a question, and indeed provides us with the answer, in 'The Hunting of the Snark':

> *'What's the good of Mercator's North Poles and Equators,*
> *Tropics, Zones and Meridian Lines?'*
> *So the Bellman would cry: and the crew would reply*
> *'They are merely conventional signs'.*

One important conventional feature of the globe not on the Bellman's list, however, is an imaginary zig-zag line that staggers drunkenly down the middle of the Pacific Ocean. It is called the International Date Line, and its purpose is very clear indeed: it is a chronological barrier to protect Tuesdays from inconvenient confrontation with any neighbouring Wednesdays.

The need for a Date Line became apparent at the International Meridian Conference in 1884 at which Greenwich Mean Time was formally adopted as the benchmark from which all other standard times throughout the world were measured. By this arrangement, the world is divided into 24 time zones of 15 degrees of longitude, corresponding to the 24 hours of the day. Moving east from Greenwich, you add an hour every 15 degrees, and moving west you subtract an hour in the same way.

But if you think about it, you realise that all these hourly increments of time, side by side encircling the globe, cannot go on for ever. Anyone travelling in a westerly direction must subtract an hour every 15 degrees, but if this arrangement were carried to its ultimate conclusion, a person travelling fast enough right around the world would end up back where he started, but on the day before. Obviously someone had to draw the line – and draw it they did at the Meridian Conference, directly opposite the 'prime' Greenwich meridian, at 180 degrees either east or west.

When crossing the International Date Line you not only change the hour, as you would when moving from one time zone to another, but the date as well. Moving from east to west, the date becomes one day later, 16 August instantly becoming 17 August; crossing eastwards, you must retard your calendar by a day.

The Date Line does not follow the 180-degree meridian exactly, but deviates here and there to avoid land areas, or to avoid splitting up the islands of a politically integrated archipelago, thereby keeping confusion in the affairs of everyday life in Oceania to a minimum. Heading south from the North Pole along 180 degrees, the Date Line takes a sudden lurch to the east through the Bering Straight to avoid separating the Chukotsky Peninsula from the rest of Russia. Then it veers for a time an equal distance to the west, to include the Aleutian Islands with Alaska. South of the equator, the line shoots out to 172.5 degrees west, but when it gets south of New Zealand it reverts again, proceeding innocently southwards along 180 degrees as if nothing whatever had happened on the way.

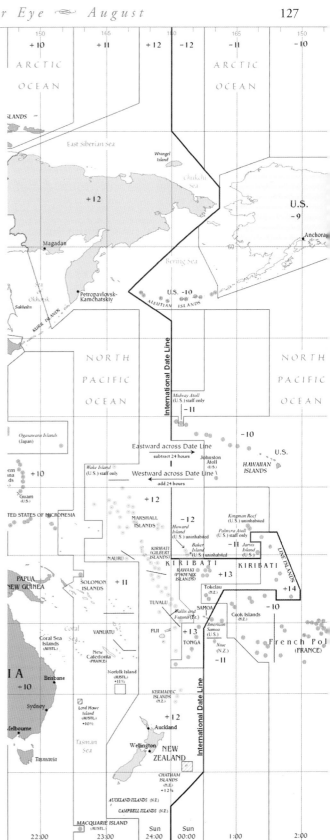

International Time Zones
Wikipedia, Creative Commons

Poetry in the Clouds

17 August 2005

The first serious attempt to classify clouds and give them names was by the French naturalist Jean Lamarck in 1802. He proposed five main divisions: hazy, massed, dappled, broom-like and grouped. But the Latin nomenclature devised shortly afterwards by the English amateur meteorologist Luke Howard has proved to be more popular and more enduring.

When the weather is calm and warm, for example, surface heating by sunshine produces ascending columns of air, here, there and yonder around the countryside. If the atmosphere is somewhat humid, cloud forms near the top of each of these invisible pillars – a bulbous, rounded cloud with a flat base, resembling a clump of cottonwool. This is a cumulus cloud, and meteorologists and literary experts alike are unanimous in the view that when William Wordsworth reclined pensively on his couch contemplating a cloud 'that floats on high o'er vales and hills', it was fair-weather cumulus he had in mind.

Shelley, on the other hand, is the cirrus expert, observing in 'Ode to the West Wind'

> *. . . even from the dim verge*
> *Of the horizon to the zenith's height,*
> *The locks of the approaching storm.*

Cirrus clouds look like tufts of hair – hence their name from the Latin word 'to curl'. They are wispy, fibrous filaments of brilliant white, too thin to cast a distinct shadow or to blur the outline of the sun or moon. These are the familiar 'mare's tails' that often stand out in bright contrast to the brilliant blue of an otherwise cloudless sky, but are the precursors of an advancing weather front – hence Shelley's 'locks of the approaching storm'.

Cirrostratus cloud is similar in texture to cirrus, but it forms a continuous sheet, a thin, diaphanous curtain drawn some 20,000 feet above the ground which hides a wan sun attempting to shine faintly through it. Cirrocumulus, on the other hand, another close relation, is rather more patchy in appearance than the other two, and

Study of Cirrus Clouds, c.1822 (oil on paper), John Constable (1776–1837)
Victoria & Albert Museum, London, UK/The Bridgeman Art Library

comprises closely spaced 'pebbly' elements, resembling cobblestones or fish-scales.

Altocumulus and stratocumulus look alike, and are distinguished mainly by their height. The former is typically 7,000 or 8,000 feet above ground level, while stratocumulus is much lower – approximately half that height. Both are a whitish grey in colour, with 'rolls' or undulations, often arranged in long, straight horizontal 'furrows'. Both are common on a dry cloudy day, where there is no particular threat of rain – but not much sun apparent either.

Altostratus, however, brings a definite threat of rain. It is normally associated with a front, and appears at first as a uniform layer of grey, relatively thin cloud, but thickens rapidly as the rain approaches. And the very lowest cloud, stratus, is the cloud you see clinging to the mountaintops in soft drizzly weather, or scurrying across the sky in ragged patches on a wet and windy day.

That Which We Call a Cloud . . .

18 August 2005

'What's in a name?' asks Juliet:

> *that which we call a rose*
> *By any other name would smell as sweet.*

Why then, one might wonder, do meteorologists have such long, pretentious and exotic names for the different types of cloud they can identify?

The reasons are largely historical. For one thing, when the system was devised back in 1802, the use of Latin made the system very adaptable for international use, since that language was the lingua franca among the intelligentsia of the time. And secondly, by following the methodology of Carl Linnaeus, whose basic principles for the scientific classification of plants and animals are still in use, Luke Howard, who devised the cloud taxonomy, ensured that any cloud described in this way could be visualised by any other meteorologist, anywhere in the world; in other words, the system is precise.

Linnaeus's system dates from the mid-1700s. The Swedish botanist grouped animal and plant species resembling each other into a genus, related genera comprised an 'order', and a group of similar orders formed a 'class'; then as regards nomenclature, each species had (at least) a double name made up of the genus and the species. Thus in the genus 'cats' we find *Felis domesticus*, the common pussycat, and *Felis leo,* the majestic lion; *Canis lupus,* meanwhile, is the European wolf, while *Canis familiaris,* as its name implies, is the familiar dog.

Howard, following the same logic, assigned to each cloud type a Latin name according to its general appearance. *Cirrus,* meaning 'curl', was used to describe wispy, fibrous strands; *cumulus* or 'heap' was ascribed to flat-based 'heap-clouds' extending upwards through the atmosphere; and *stratus*, 'spread out', was the label attached to horizontal sheets. These three primary categories in various combinations, with the addition of *alto,* meaning high, and *nimbus,* a cloud, became the basis for the ten main cloud families, corresponding to Linnaeus's genera: *cirrus*, *cirrocumulus* and *cirrostratus*; *altocumulus, altostratus* and *nimbostratus*; and *stratus, stratocumulus, cumulus* and *cumulonimbus.*

Then, within each genus, are the species, which may again be differentiated on the basis of their shape or structure, or perhaps the physical process in which a particular cloud has had its origin. There are 14 species altogether, with names like *fibratus* (composed of filaments), *congestus* (sprouting upwards), *floccus* (composed of tufts), or *fractus* (meaning 'ragged'). And then there are 'varieties', which describe – in Latin, naturally – further characteristics of an individual cloud.

So told by a colleague, for example, of a fine display of *Altocumulus stratiformis translucidus,* a meteorologist will immediately visualise a shallow, spreading layer of cloud, perhaps 8,000 feet above the ground, through which the position of the sun can be easily discerned.

Cloud study, 1981-862/1, c.1803-1811 (pink and grey wash), **Luke Howard (1772–1864),** *Light cirrocumulus beneath cirrus. Inscribed in pencil: Cirrus,* Royal Meteorological Society

An Angry Summer in the Bee-Loud Glade

23 August 2005

'*Sic vos non vobis mellificatis apes*,' said Virgil, no doubt having thought about it deeply for some time. At first glance the poet might seem to be telling a tribe of well-intentioned chimpanzees that he was sick of them. But no; Virgil here addresses honey bees, and compliments them on their generosity. 'You bees,' he declares mellifluously, 'do not make your honey for yourselves,' the implication being, I suppose, that the bees must make their honey for us humans.

But even the most generous of honey bees, like us, may get annoyed at times. As a general rule, it happens only when their hive is under threat, but when that threat exists, as any expert at Dublin's current Apimondia will tell you, the bees can turn aggressive. Strangely enough, however, they will defend the hive more vigorously in some weather conditions than they will in others. This was discovered by two otherwise respected members of the American university fraternity who spent the long, hot summer of 1987 provoking honey bees.

Their *modus operandi* was relatively simple. Having found a beehive, they would remove the lid and lower into it a little black bag made of leather. After a short while they would extract the bag, replace the lid, collect their bits and pieces and repair forthwith to the next beehive on their list.

It was a well-planned operation. The unfortunate insects had first been provoked to anger by the infiltration into the hive of a substance called isopentyl acetate, which apparently acts like a red rag to a bee. The leather bags were 'targets', which the angry insects then attacked, and when the targets had been subjected to bombardment for precisely 15 seconds, they were withdrawn from the hive and the number of stings was counted. At the same time, of course, all the usual weather parameters were faithfully recorded.

The experiment was also carefully controlled in other ways. The pilgrimage from hive to hive was necessary to eliminate a phenomenon which we scientists always refer to as 'genetic intercolonial variation', the well-known tendency for bees in some colonies to lose the rag rather more quickly than they do in others. Moreover, each individual hive was re-tested at five- to seven-day intervals, this being the period which is scientifically reckoned to be necessary for an angry bee to cool down after having been provoked.

By the end of the summer the pair had reached conclusions. The number of bee stings, it seems, was found to be positively related to levels of temperature, humidity, barometric pressure and solar radiation, and negatively related to wind speed. In other words, the bees were at their most aggressive on hot, sunny and humid days when there was very little wind.

All extremely interesting, of course, but one cannot help feeling that the bees must have been greatly relieved when the new academic year at last began.

Man Catching Bees,
14th century
British Library

The Dance of the Honey Bee

24 August 2005

Honey bees are very clever creatures. Some say they can even make their own weather forecasts, and plan their work accordingly:

> *When bees to distance wing their flight*
> *Days are warm and skies are bright;*
> *But when their flight ends near their home*
> *Stormy weather is sure to come.*

But bees, it seems, are even cleverer than this. Having decided that the weather is set fair, and having proceeded some distance from the hive and found a promising source of much-prized nectar, the resourceful honeybee then shares this information with its hive-mates. Aristotle was aware of this ability, but had no idea how it was achieved. Pliny the Elder tried to find out by incorporating in his hive a window made of transparent horn through which he could observe the bees' behaviour; he noticed that returning bees would often do a little dance, but did not speculate as to its purpose. It was left to a German expert, Karl von Frisch, to unlock the secret of this dance in 1943.

The dance of the returning bee is performed on the vertical surface of a hanging honeycomb. The insect follows a path which resembles two capital Ds laid front to front and pushed together, or if you prefer, an oval shape with a short-cut from one long side to the other. Along this imaginary track the successful forager traces out a figure-of-eight pattern, and waggles itself in dance-like fashion each time it negotiates the 'short-cut'.

The direction in which the dancer faces during her waggling stint is all-important; it indicates the direction of the food-source in relation to the direction of the sun. Thus, if the bee waggles when facing straight up towards the top of the hive, towards 12 o'clock if you like, the food will be found exactly in the direction of the sun; if she faces downwards, towards 6 o'clock, during her waggle, the food is in the opposite direction from the sun; and if she faces 60 degrees away from the vertical, say towards

2 o'clock, then the food in the real world outside the hive lies in a direction 60 degrees to the right of the sun. Meanwhile, the distance from the hive to the food is proportional to the vigour of the dance; the closer the food, the more enthusiastic the Terpsichorean gyrations of the insect.

Finally, when the bee has finished her dance, she dispenses to her audience small samples of what she has collected, so that her sister bees can judge for themselves the quality of the food whose location they have been apprised of. If they approve, many of the watcher bees will visit the source, return to the hive, and do a little dance themselves, thus initiating a new wave of foragers. Eventually the best food sources inspire the most dances, and are therefore visited by the most bees.

Nova 2644 fol.94v Beehives, from 'Tacuinum Sanitatis' (vellum),
Italian School *(14th century)*
Osterreichische Nationalbibliothek,
Vienna, Austria/Alinari
The Bridgeman Art Library

The Horologion of Andronicus of Kyrrhos

6 September 2005

'There is no end to this city,' wrote Cicero about Athens in the first century BC: 'Everywhere you step you are confronted with the past.' From my experience over recent days I can report Cicero's observation still valid after two millennia. The city is dominated by the sacred rock of the Acropolis; from there one can gaze down upon the Areopagus, the Supreme Court of ancient Athens. Farther to the west, the hill of Pnyx was the gathering place of the Athenian citizens where democracy first found its voice. But of most interest to meteorologists, close by the Acropolis overlooking the old Athenian marketplace is the Horologion of Andronicus of Kyrrhos, known as the 'Tower of the Winds'.

The ancient Greeks personified the winds, imagining each as a named person endowed with the characteristics brought to mind by the breezes blowing from the various quarters of their world. Notos, for example, was the wind from the south, and was a sticky, slimy person; when portrayed in a picture or a sculpture he was provided with all the hallmarks of the excessive moisture he acquired on his passage to Greece across the Mediterranean. The cold northerly wind was Boreas, a bearded old man, warmly clothed and holding a shell near his mouth into which he blew to make his howling noise. Kaikias, the northeasterly, was portrayed holding an upturned shield half-full of hailstones, as if he were ready to rattle them down on the surrounding countryside. The other winds were also appropriately personified – like Apeliotes, the showery east wind, and Zephros, the gentle westerly.

During Cicero's lifetime, the inhabitants of Athens commissioned Andronicus of Kyrrhos to build a structure to depict these eight important persons. The result was the Tower of the Winds, an octagonal marble structure 42 feet high and 26 feet in diameter. It had eight faces, each embellished with a sculpted figure representing one of these mythical personifications, and the roof was originally surmounted by a weather-vane so that citizens, by noting the position of the vane relative to the sculpted figures, could avail themselves of a simple short-term weather forecast.

But the tower had a second function, as indicated by the name *horologion:* it told the time. In sunny weather, the time was indicated by a series of sundials incised on the marble of the external walls of the building. And for cloudy conditions, the structure incorporated a water-lock or *clepsydra*, comprising a large container of water, which was allowed to empty slowly and steadily through a small hole, similar in principle to the familiar hourglass.

The Tower of Andronicus is still there, albeit less imposing than it used to be. It has lost its wind vane and is somewhat weatherbeaten, but the structure itself with the carved figures of the Grecian winds survives, a fitting monument to the meteorology of ancient Greece.

Skiron (North West)

Boreas (North)

Zephyros (West)

Kaikias (North East)

Lips (South West)

Notos (South)

Evros (South East)

Apeliotes (East)

Set of eight Greek stamps showing the eight winds depicted on the Horologion of Andronicus

All the Fullness of Time

9 September 2005

The American writer Henry D. Thoreau has described us all as standing at the meeting point of two eternities: one past, the other yet to come. Within this profound and infinite context, however, we humans have always been conscious of the fact that time moves on; even without means of telling what the hour may be, we are conscious of travelling steadily from the past into the future. But as Jacques remarks in *As You Like It*: 'Time travels in divers paces with divers persons'.

The rate at which *tempus* appears to *fugit* for the individual depends on many things. It ticks by slowly, for example, if we are bored, like T.S. Eliot's J. Alfred Prufrock, who famously 'measured out my life with coffee spoons'. When we are engaged in something we enjoy, however, the hours slip by unnoticed.

Other factors also play a part. Research suggests that the more often a task is broken up, or the more frequently it is interrupted, the longer will seem to us the time required for its completion. Moreover, relatively passive activities seem to take longer than those requiring active participation; at a lecture, for example, time passes more quickly for those who take down copious notes than it does for those who simply sit and listen to the speaker without actually doing anything themselves.

Studies into many other *temps perdu* conclude, as one's personal experience might well suggest, that the level of motivation is important; the more enthusiastic one is about a given task, the shorter the time it seems to take for its completion. More subtly we are told that 'time has subjective duration only when it is the object of attention'; we become impatient waiting for a tardy spouse, for example, but are oblivious to time as we joyously celebrate his or her eventual arrival. It all adds up to 'time flies when you're having fun'.

There is no detectable difference, it seems, between the way in which men and women perceive time – but age is all-important. Children find it hard to give a reasonably accurate, objective measure of duration; presumably, through inexperience, they are less able than adults to compensate first-guess perceptions to take account of the differences in nature between boring and exciting tasks, or for differences in personal motivation. Elderly people, on the other hand, tend to estimate an interval of time as shorter than it really was – probably because, with the ennui of age, they are less likely to be distracted by extraneous happenings to which they have been long accustomed.

Marcel Proust summed it all up very well in *À la recherche du temps perdu*: 'The time which we have at our disposal every day is elastic,' he wrote. 'The passions that we feel expand it, those that we inspire contract it; and habit fills up whatever interval remains.'

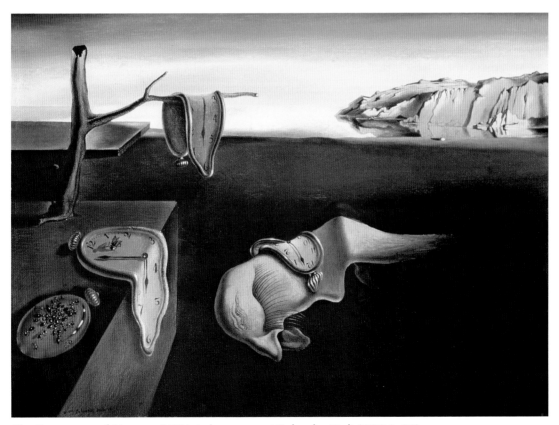

The Persistence of Memory, 1931 (oil on canvas), Salvador Dali (1904–89)
Museum of Modern Art, New York, USA/The Bridgeman Art Library

Sir Sloshua and the Belt of Venus

10 September 2005

When Sir Joshua Reynolds died
All Nature was degraded;
The King dropped a tear in the Queen's ear,
And all his pictures faded.

By this little rhyme, the Romantic poet William Blake whimsically described one of the greatest flaws in Joshua Reynolds's *oeuvre*. Sir Joshua, although President of the Royal Academy and the foremost portrait painter of the eighteenth century, was sometimes injudicious in his choices of materials and his techniques. Inspired by a two-year visit to Italy in his late twenties, he tried to reproduce the delicate effects of Titian and Tintoretto. In this he was partially successful, but the pigments he used for his flesh tones turned out to be unstable, and many of his paintings faded, even during his lifetime, leaving many of his subjects with a deathly pallor.

Reynolds was also ridiculed by more *avant-garde* practitioners of the nineteenth century, like John Everett Millais and Dante Gabriel Rosetti, for the traditional lack of detail in the backgrounds of his paintings. These stalwarts of the so-called Pre-Raphaelite Brotherhood believed every detail of a scene to have significance, and painted everything into sharp focus; Reynolds, by contrast, and following the practice of his time, would provide detail only in the foreground and simplify the background. The Pre-Raphaelites coined the term 'sloshy' to describe this allegedly *passé* technique, and the sobriquet 'Sir Sloshua' to identify its most illustrious proponent.

Sir Sloshua's fuzzy background is nowhere more evident than in *Cupid Unfastening the Girdle of Venus*. The nondescript backdrop to the scene portrayed in the painting focuses our attention on a chubby little cherub who sits beside the Roman goddess who is reclining in her *déshabillé;* the cherub is, well, doing exactly what it says on the label. To meteorologists, however, the 'belt of Venus' is something altogether more mundane and less *risqué,* and has nothing to do with either the goddess or the planet.

On an evening when the sky is cloudless and the weather hazy, it is sometimes possible to see, just after sunset, the shadow of the Earth projected against the sky over the eastern horizon. It appears as a dark, bluish-grey horizontal band rising slowly upwards shortly after the sun in the west has disappeared. The more hazy the atmosphere, the better it acts as a screen on to which this shadow is projected.

High up, of course, the sky will still be its normal colour blue, displaying perhaps a slightly pinkish tinge as often happens after sunset. But in between this brighter area of blue and the dark, eastern shadow down below, is a narrow band – a horizontal fringe to the shadow, as it were – which is a very definite shade of reddish brown. It is caused by the scattering by the atmosphere of the red light of the setting sun in the direction of the observer, and is called the 'belt of Venus'.

Cupid Unfastening the Girdle of Venus, 1788 (oil on canvas), **Sir Joshua Reynolds (1723–92)** Hermitage, St. Petersburg, Russia The Bridgeman Art Library

Shine On, Harvest Moon

17 September 2005

Autumn is well and truly with us now. As the poet James Thomson put it, accurately but awkwardly, nearly 300 years ago:

> *The western Sun withdraws the shortened day;*
> *And humid Evening, gliding o'er the sky,*
> *In her chill progress, to the ground condensed*
> *The vapours throws.*

And then he goes on to describe a phenomenon very noticeable at this time of year:

> *. . . Meanwhile the Moon,*
> *Full-orbed, and breaking through the scattered clouds,*
> *Shews her broad visage in the crimsoned east,*
>
> *. . . . .*
> *. . . and sheds a softer day.*

Thomson was referring to the Harvest Moon, which you will see tonight, weather permitting, peeping above the eastern horizon shortly after sunset.

Now, there are misconceptions about the Harvest Moon. As Rev. T.F. Thiselton Dyer has pointed out in his *English Folk-lore,* written in 1878: 'There is a very prevalent opinion among the lower and uneducated classes that the Harvest Moon always occurs at the time of harvest, let that happen when it may. It is needless, however, to remark that such an erroneous idea can only proceed from persons of an entirely ignorant turn of mind – it being childish to suppose that a change of the moon could in any way be influenced by such an occurrence.'

We may feel uneasy at the turn of phrase which flows so trippingly from his reverence's pen, but we must defend to the death the logic of his main thrust. Harvest Moon is simply the name given to the full moon which occurs nearest to the autumn equinox, around 22 September, since it was the custom in days gone by for farmers to take advantage of the succession of bright moonlit evenings it provided to gather in the last of their late crops.

The prominence of the Harvest Moon is related to the fact that the September full moon rises above the horizon at about the same time each evening, coinciding almost exactly with the setting sun. Moonrise throughout the lunar cycle occurs a little later each day by an amount of time known as the retardation. The mean value of the retardation is about 50 minutes, but it varies; it is at its maximum of well over an hour around the time of the vernal equinox, and at a minimum in the autumn. At this time of year, therefore, it seems to the casual observer that the full moon rises at the same time each evening – almost, as it were, taking over from the sun.

Because of its position low in the sky near the horizon, the early evening Harvest Moon appears much larger than usual, but its bigness is an illusion. Instrumental measurements show that the moon's angular size, whatever the time of year, does not vary significantly whether viewed near the horizon or approaching its zenith. What varies is our perception of its size, influenced in the former case by the angular proximity of familiar terrestrial objects.

Coming From Evening Church, 1830 (mixed media),
Samuel Palmer (1805–81) © Tate Gallery

Ruminations on the Rive Gauche

27 September 2005

Today's *Weather Eye* comes from the Rue Dauphine, a very narrow little rue indeed on the Rive Gauche in Paris. Outside on the noisy street, little Peugeots and Renaults are parked end to end, and every so often an owner repossesses his vehicle in the traditional Parisian mode – by none-too-carefully nudging the cars to his fore and aft sufficiently out of the way to allow him egress. Meanwhile, my family has departed to view the *Winged Victory* and the *Venus of Milo* in the Louvre, there too, no doubt, to be recaptivated by the magnificent insignificance of Leonardo's *Mona Lisa.*

It has been said that Leonardo arranged for music to be played while he painted the *Mona Lisa,* so that her countenance might retain the rapt demeanour from which the painting derives its haunting, enigmatic charm. In meteorological circles, however, the *Mona Lisa* is noted for another reason; it is allegedly the first Renaissance painting in which the sky is hazy. Artworks theretofore had portrayed the sky with perfect visibility, but the steep mountains of the *Mona Lisa,* with their strange perspectives and mysterious waterways, are viewed through a misty or hazy atmosphere, which adds a luminous quality to the entire work.

Although Leonardo achieved recognition in his lifetime as a painter, a sculptor and an architect, it was only long after his death that it was discovered, from his secret notebooks, that he also had a gift for science. In 1495, for example, he produced a sketch of a person floating in the sky and wearing what appears to be a kind of parachute. But it was here in Paris in 1797 that Leonardo's concept was transformed into something like reality.

In October that year, one André-Jacques Garnerin was arrested as a swindler because he had charged spectators to watch balloon ascents, and some of his balloons refused to fly. The police, however, in a novel precursor to 'community service', released the would-be aviator under bond, either to perform a promised jump from a balloon or go to jail.

Citizen Garnerin's balloon took off from the Parc de Monceau – across the river not too far from where I sit – and he began his descent from 700 metres. His 'parachute' was a small gondola, suspended by strings from a flimsy canopy of thin material, and according to one onlooker: 'The machine made quite enormous oscillations; the air, gathering and compressed under it, would sometimes escape by one side, sometimes by the other, thus shaking and whirling the parachute about with a violence which, however great, had happily no unfortunate effect.'

And so, down to Earth came André-Jacques. He survived many more spectacular descents until finally, in August 1823, he received a blow from the wooden rigging of a balloon as he prepared for take-off – a contretemps, alas, which proved to be *le commencement de la fin* for M. Garnerin.

Side view of the Victory of Samothrace
(Parian marble)
Louvre, Paris, France/Peter Willi
The Bridgeman Art Library

The Purpose of the Pendulum

28 September 2005

This morning I rose early and walked with my son, Stephen, up the Boulevard Saint-Michel to the Rue Soufflot, and there before us in all its glory was the Panthéon. Architecturally in the classical tradition, the building was once a church, but was transformed during the Revolution into a collective tomb for the distinguished or heroic French. Mirabeau was the first to be buried in the crypt, followed by the ashes of Voltaire and Rousseau, and more recently by Victor Hugo, the Curies, and the Resistance leader Jean Moulin.

But the nave belongs to Foucault's pendulum. I have seen it many times before, of course, but it has become for me something of a pilgrimage each time we visit Paris to reassure myself, as it were, that the planet is still revolving safely on its axis. For that, indeed, is the purpose of the pendulum. Following the gradual acceptance of the Copernican system of astronomy during the seventeenth and eighteenth centuries, virtually everyone agreed that Earth revolves, but no one was able to prove it until Jean Bernard Léon Foucault came along. This he did in front of an invited audience in 1851 by means of the vast pendulum suspended from inside the Panthéon's dome.

The concept is easier to understand if you imagine a pendulum over the North Pole – a heavy weight swinging to and fro at the end of a long string. As the pendulum swings back and forth, the Earth rotates beneath it, anti-clockwise. Since the plane of oscillation of the pendulum stays fixed in space, the path traced by the moving weight will appear to rotate clockwise, completing a full revolution every 24 hours.

The matter is more complex at lower latitudes. Theory predicts that the plane of oscillation of the pendulum should still rotate, but that it will take a much longer time to complete a full revolution. In any event, the changing path of the moving weight is conclusive proof that the Earth rotates beneath it; the Panthéon, in fact, revolves around the pendulum, not vice versa.

Le pendule de Foucault comprises a golden sphere hanging by a wire that is 67 metres long; on the floor, a large, white ring surrounds the zone of oscillation, and is marked with a series of numerals with which to gauge the slow precession of the pendulum. I timed its motion, found that it took 8 seconds to move from side to side, then did the calculations based on the stated length of the suspending wire, and

Foucault's Pendulum, photos.com

found that the period, the time it took to go to and fro and to again, should be 16.47 seconds. I thereby found myself doubly reassured both that the Earth revolves, and that the Law of the Simple Pendulum appears to be correct.

And I have gone upon my way, strangely in awe of this great world in which we live.

The Retreat of the Glaciers

8 October 2005

Aglacier is more than just a massive wedge of solid water. It lives, it moves, it grows or may decay; it flows along a mountain valley like a frozen river in full flood, trapped in a time-warp of perpetual slow motion. At times, indeed, the powerful progress of a glacier can be seen and heard, with awestruck observers aware of violent tremblings underfoot.

They can move at quite surprising speeds. In its heyday, the steep, short Glacier des Bossons at Chamonix would edge forward with remarkable consistency at a speed of nearly 600 feet per year, a regularity which made possible one of the most macabre long-range forecasts of all time. In 1820, several climbers were swept into the des Bossons by an avalanche; the Scottish glaciologist James Forbes predicted they would emerge from the foot of the glacier in 35 to 40 years, and 41 years later, more or less on schedule, the glacier duly surrendered the bodies of the mountaineers.

Glacier ice either advances or retreats. One century may be characterised by the advance of glaciers from their mountain fastnesses onto the fertile plains of valleys down below; the next may be one of steady glacier retreat. Advance or retreat depends on the balance existing between the accumulation of snow in the glacier's upper reaches, and the ablation – or melting away – that occurs near the 'snout' or head, the inter-connection being the erratic movement of the glacier itself. Both are greatly affected by any change in climate, although the response of the glacier may lag behind by several decades.

There is much concern at present that virtually all the world's glaciers seem to be in organised retreat. Satellite images show glaciers receding in Patagonia, the Himalayas, the Alps and Pyrenees; here in Europe, only in Norway, where shifting weather patterns have led to larger snowfalls, do glaciers seem to be holding their own or even tending to advance. Global warming is being blamed, and although this explanation becomes more valid as the years go by, the issue has been much more complex.

The fact is that the world's glaciers have been retreating for more than 150 years since they reached their maximum coverage around the middle of the nineteenth century. The most generally accepted theory is that the retreat began as a response to the climatic recovery from the Little Ice Age, an intensely cold period lasting several centuries which ended around the time of the observed peak in glacial extent. But any retreat owing to this climatic recovery should have tailed off long ago, and indeed, in the case of many glaciers, net melting ceased around the middle of the twentieth century, only to resume with a vengeance around 1980. Global warming, largely brought about by the enhanced greenhouse effect, is widely acknowledged to have been the most important factor in the observed retreat of the glaciers since then.

The Source of the Arveyron, 1781 (pen and ink and watercolour on paper), **Francis Towne** (1739–1816)
© Tate Gallery

The Waters of the World

11 October 2005

Earth is unique in the solar system in having a surface temperature so delicately balanced that water can exist simultaneously in all its three states: liquid, solid and gas. Some of our sister worlds are far too hot for liquid seas, and worlds more distant from the Sun eke out their existence in perennial ice. Earth is the only planet that we know of to have vast bodies of liquid water exposed to the atmosphere above.

In one sense the oceans are vast. They have an area of 140 million square miles, cover 71 per cent of the Earth's surface, and account for 97 per cent of the planet's water. They have a total volume of some 300 cubic miles, and an average depth of two and a half miles.

But looked at in another way the sea is less impressive. The oceans comprise only a tiny fraction of the Earth's volume. If we were to imagine the Earth as a billiard ball, the ocean would be an almost unnoticeable film of dampness on its surface; and if you were to make your way to its very deepest spot, you would have descended only 1/600th part of the total distance to the centre of the Earth.

It used to be thought that the ocean bed was flat and featureless, a smooth receptacle for all this surplus water. But around the middle of the last century, when it was decided to lay a telegraphic cable across the North Atlantic, its topography became a matter of some practical importance. By repeatedly paying out miles of weighted cable until it reached the bottom, the scientists of the day discovered that the Atlantic Ocean was shallower in the middle than it was at either side. They named the shallow region in the centre 'Telegraph Plateau' to commemorate the great endeavour which led to its discovery.

But further surprises lay in store. The invention of echo-sounding in the early 1920s showed that Telegraph Plateau was not the gentle rise and fall of ground it seemed to be, but a massive mountain range, much longer and more rugged than anything on land. It ran down the entire length of the Atlantic, its highest peaks breaking through the surface of the water to become islands like Ascension, the Azores and Tristan da Cunha. So in 1925 they renamed it the 'Mid-Atlantic Ridge'.

Then later soundings showed that the Ridge was not confined to the Atlantic. It curves around Africa and moves up the western side of the Indian Ocean to Arabia, while part of it curves southwards around Australia and New Zealand to perform a majestic whirl in the Pacific. And it was not a perfect ridge at all; it has a deep canyon running along its crest throughout its entire length, a canyon which, with understandable hyperbole, has come to be called the Great Global Rift.

Terceira, engraved by **Edward Finden,** *after a painting by* **Warren Henry (1794–1879),** Private Collection/Bridgeman Art Library

Hotspur and a Holy Day of Horrors

1 November 2005

Diseased nature oftentimes breaks forth
In strange eruptions; oft the teeming earth
Is with a kind of colic pinched and vexed,
By the imprisoning of unruly wind
Within her womb; which for enlargement striving
Shakes the old beldame earth and topples down
Steeples and moss-grown towers.

Hotspur's interesting theory, outlined in Shakespeare's *Henry IV, Part 1,* seemed to become reality in Portugal on 1 November 1755. On the morning of All Saints' Day 250 years ago, the sky over Lisbon was bright and cloudless, and the churches were thronged with worshippers to mark the holy day. Suddenly, and without warning, at 9.45am, two violent earth tremors shook the city to its foundations.

Rows of houses fell like dominoes, chasms yawned in the streets, and churches collapsed on their congregations. An onlooker some distance out to sea described the entire city as 'waving to and fro like a wind-blown field of corn'. Residents rushed from the narrow streets towards hoped-for refuge on the waterfront only to see the waters of the Tagus first recede towards the sea, and then return in three great waves that smashed the sea wall and penetrated deep into the heart of the ruined city.

Meanwhile, candles that had been lit in homes and churches to mark the holy day set the remaining buildings ablaze. Of the 275,000 inhabitants of Lisbon at that time, some 15,000 died immediately in the devastation of the tremors and the tidal waves which followed; perhaps twice that number succumbed to the fire, or to disease and other hardships in the aftermath.

The epicentre of the quake had not been below Lisbon itself, but in the Atlantic some hundreds of kilometres to the west of Portugal. Although seismographs had yet to be invented, contemporary descriptions have allowed the tremor to be estimated at 8.7 on the Richter scale; this makes it the largest earthquake ever to have occurred in Europe, and some 30 times more powerful than the one which destroyed San Francisco in 1906.

Lisbon, 1755, G.M. Burghry
Jan Kosak Collection

The tragedy did, however, lay the foundations of the science of seismology. The king's chief minister, the Marquis de Pombal, ordered information to be collected about the effects of the earthquake in every parish in Portugal. This data on, *inter alia,* the duration of the tremors and the heights of the tsunamis made possible the first rigorous analysis of an earthquake, and prompted the scientists of the day to investigate the causes of such phenomena. The exercise culminated five years later in a paper by John Michell in the English journal *Philosophical Transactions of the Royal Society,* in which were described for the first time, and with a great deal more insight than that displayed by Harry Hotspur, the likely causes of major earthquakes.

A Queen of Indiscretion

2 November 2005

On 2 November 1755, the day after the Lisbon earthquake whose 250th anniversary we commemorated yesterday, a daughter was born in Vienna to the Empress Maria Theresa and her husband, the Holy Roman Emperor Francis I. She was christened Maria Antonia and in 1770 she married the Dauphin Louis, grandson of King Louis XV of France. The Dauphin in due course became Louis XVI, and Maria Antonia achieved an unenviable place in history as the ill-fated Queen Marie-Antoinette.

Frivolous, imprudent and prodigal, Marie-Antoinette's behaviour contributed in no small way to the popular unrest that led to the Revolution. Most famously insensitive, perhaps, was her apocryphal remark in 1789, 'Let them eat cake,' or more probably something like '*Qu'ils mangent de la brioche*,' allegedly reflecting her naive assumption that the poor of Paris, having no bread, had as wide a choice of alternative food as she had.

But they did not. Bread at that time was, quite literally, a vital commodity to the poorer classes of French society. Indeed, their entire diet was composed of cereal in one form or another, either as bread, gruel, or some form of liquid broth. If a harvest was poor, matters were very serious indeed; it meant famine in the countryside and severe shortage in the cities, where subsistence depended on the availability of grain at reasonable prices. The dependence of the populace on grain resembled that of the Irish on the potato some years later.

As it happened, poor harvests, brought on by lack of rain, were a common feature of the eighteenth century in France. The meteorological records show that 1709, 1725, 1749 and 1775 were years of very low rainfall. The same was true of 1785, when once again there was very little rain and agricultural yields were low. But 1788 was worst of all; an exceptionally warm spring began a year which turned out to be the driest of the decade, and the resulting drought was followed by the worst harvest for many years.

The rise in the price of wheat and rye began in March 1788 in anticipation of this poor harvest. It continued inexorably over the next 15 months, and the graph, coincidentally or otherwise, reaches a peak exactly in July 1789, the month of the fall of the Bastille, when the price of bread was 75 per cent higher than it had been a year before. As a result, civil disturbance brought on by lack of food grew commonplace throughout the kingdom, famine stalked the land, and in the towns and cities the high price of bread caused riots in the streets.

Neither Marie-Antoinette nor the weather directly caused the Revolution, but in the late 1780s both in their own way contributed to the popular unrest, to the great discontent of the angry citizens of Paris, and to the extreme violence of the events that followed.

A Woman Baking Bread, 1854 (oil on canvas), **Jean-François Millet (1814–75)** Collection Kröller-Müller Museum, Otterlo, the Netherlands

The Old Moon in the New Moon's Arms

4 November 2005

Given clear skies, the full Moon is always spectacularly conspicuous. But it is much harder to be aware of a new Moon, for the simple reason that at that point in the cycle no lunar presence is visible in the sky at all. After a day or so, however, as is happening at present, a thin, bright crescent appears, and at that time the outline of the remainder of the lunar disc can be dimly seen on a clear night – as is sometimes said, 'the old moon in the new moon's arms'. This faint illumination is called 'earthshine', a consequence of sunlight reflected towards the lunar surface from the Earth. It is only noticeable when there is so little of the sunlit portion visible that its light does not overwhelm the much dimmer earthshine.

Leonardo da Vinci was the first to twig what earthshine was. He described it in considerable detail around 1510, with diagrams to illustrate his point, in the document which has come to be known as the *Codex Leicester* and which has received much notoriety of late for the prominent part it plays in Dan Brown's novel *The Da Vinci Code*. The *Codex* contains a section entitled 'Of the Moon: No Solid Body is Lighter than Air', and in this Leonardo states his belief that the Moon has an atmosphere and also oceans; he believed the Moon was a good reflector of light because it was covered with so much water. He was also of the view that earthshine, or 'the ghostly glow' as he called it, was due to sunlight reflected from the Earth's oceans subsequently hitting the moon.

Leonardo, as it happens, was wrong on two counts: as we know, there are no oceans on the moon, and secondly, it is our earthly clouds, and not our oceans, that provide the main source of reflected light for earthshine. But for him to have got the basic explanation right was a remarkable achievement in an age when most people were unaware that Earth orbited the Sun. Copernicus's Sun-centred theory of the solar system, after all, was published only in 1543, 24 years after Leonardo's death.

Because the light which causes earthshine is reflected mainly by clouds, the ghostly glow varies from month to month, and even from hour to hour. Earthshine is at its most intense – about 10 per cent brighter than average – during April and May, because total cloud cover on Earth is generally greatest around that time of year. And on any particular day, the amount of cloud presented in the direction of the Moon by the rotating Earth varies significantly throughout the 24 hours. The Pacific Ocean, for example, appears relatively dark when viewed from space, but a big cloud-covered continent like Asia appears predominantly a brilliant white, reflecting perhaps two or three times more sunlight towards the Moon than any of the oceans.

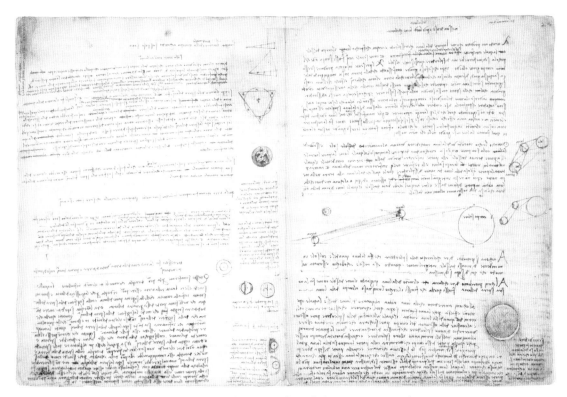

Page from Codex Leicester, showing a diagram of Earthshine amongst other items,
Leonardo da Vinci (1452–1519), Corbis

Canute Favoured by the Fetch Factor

12 November 2005

'Ocean! The land on which I sit is mine, and thou art a part of my dominion. Therefore rise not, but obey my commands, nor presume to wet even the edge of my royal robe.' Thus, according to tradition, did King Canute address the waves. Tired of the extravagant adulation of his courtiers, he had caused his golden throne to be placed on the seashore as the tide came rolling in. The incoming water, of course, took no notice of the King and he used the incident as an object lesson to demonstrate to his sycophantic followers the illusory nature of his apparent omnipotence: 'Confess now how frivolous and vain,' he said, 'is the might of an earthly king who says unto the ocean "Thus far shalt thou go and no farther".'

Canute at the time, around 1032, was the most powerful ruler in the north of Europe, his domain by then including Norway, Denmark, part of Sweden and, most recently, that part of Britain we now think of as England. But as in the case of the waves, Canute's earthly power was insufficient to prevent the inevitable; he died at Shaftesbury at the age of 39, 970 years ago today on 12 November 1035.

Assuming the waves Canute was trying to stop were somewhere on the east coast of England, the chances are they were not very high. High waves need lots of 'fetch', and for most wind directions, fetch in the North Sea is very limited. But let us start at the beginning.

In the absence of a swell – waves, as it were, rolling in from somewhere else – when there is very little wind the sea is smooth or almost so. But as a breeze picks up, tiny wavelets begin to run downwind along the surface, rather like the ripples that streak across your coffee cup as you blow on it to cool it down. The wavelets are nurtured by a waxing wind; they move in its general direction and they increase in height as time goes by. The stronger the wind, the higher the resulting waves will ultimately be.

But fetch, the distance available for waves to form, is the other factor that determines wave-height. Given enough wind, the waves will grow and grow as they travel over miles of ocean; but if fetch is limited, they have insufficient room to reach their full potential. A powerful wave breaking on the Kerry coast in a strong westerly, for example, has had an effectively infinite amount of fetch; it may have travelled thousands of miles, beginning its life several days before as a minute undulation on

Canute holding back the waves, engraving
photos.com

the balmy waters of the Caribbean. By contrast, waves formed in an easterly wind between Denmark and the coast of northern England have only a limited amount of fetch. There was a fair likelihood, therefore, that Canute could make his point without suffering the indignity of inundation.

Long Live the Skating Water Drops

22 November 2005

'*Leider nicht,*' they say in Germany when, for example, you ask in a shop for something that they do not stock. 'Sadly, no,' is the response. With this in mind, you might be forgiven for assuming that the *Leidenfrost phenomenon* was some kind of melancholy prevalent on frosty nights. But *leider nicht!* It has more to do with the way your granny used to test the frying pan before she cooked the pancakes. She would, if you remember, sprinkle on it a few drops of water, and if at first the drops just sizzled away to nothing within seconds, she knew it was not hot enough: when, on the other hand, the drops beaded up and danced for some considerable time around the metal, she knew the perfect temperature had been reached.

If the surface of the pan is warm but not too hot, simmering somewhere below 100°C, a drop of water will evaporate, and rather rapidly. At a higher temperature, say between 100 and 150°C, the water drops will boil and disappear in a little whiff of steam even more quickly than they did before. But if the pan is very hot, at around 200°C, a strange thing begins to happen: the drops of water glide serenely and gracefully around the pan, and do not evaporate for a full minute or maybe even longer.

This is the Leidenfrost phenomenon, which clearly has no connection whatever with any kind of frost. It is so called because it was discovered in 1756 by a German scientist from Duisburg called Johann Gottlob Leidenfrost, and he explained it in a learned treatise called *De Aquae Communis Nonnullis Qualitatibus Tractatus,* 'A Tract about Some Qualities of Common Water'. The drops on the very hot pan behave this way because they have acquired a little cushion of water vapour underneath to hold them a fraction of a millimetre above the surface of the metal. This insulating cushion forms only when the surface of the pan is very hot indeed, but when it does materialise it acts as an insulator to prevent further heat from flowing freely upwards into the liquid drop of water. The drops therefore skim around and around the frying pan like little tiny skaters, their longevity assured by the frictionless cushion on which each one is perched.

It is believed that the Leidenfrost effect, rather than any alleged 'mind over matter' victory, may play a part in the reported ability of some persons to walk barefoot over red hot coals. Such an accomplishment can be partly explained by the fact that if the performer strides briskly across the coals, each footfall will be so brief as to allow very little heat energy to be conducted to the feet. But if, as well, a performer's feet are wet, a layer of vaporised moisture, *à la* Leidenfrost, might provide at least a modicum of insulation.

Johann Gottlob Leidenfrost (1715–94) was a German doctor and theologian who first described the scientific phenomenon eponymously named the Leidenfrost effect.
Wikipedia Commons

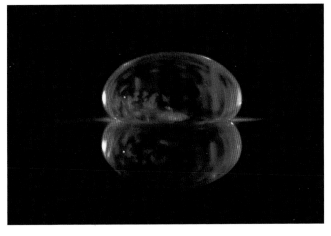

Photograph taken using a handheld digital camera at low speed approximately 5cm from the droplet.
Ilya Lisenker,
University of Colorado, Boulder

A Wind to Make the Blood Run Cold

24 November 2005

'The air bites shrewdly,' if I might borrow Hamlet's way of putting it. Or if it doesn't yet where you are, it will do so over the next few days if the forecasts are to be believed. The rationale behind these predictions of 'a nipping and an eager air' can be clearly understood by glancing at the weather map, and recalling that, for practical purposes, the wind can be regarded as flowing straight along the isobars. From this, it will be clear that the air moving southwards towards Ireland for the next few days will have originated somewhere near Spitzbergen in the Arctic, and will have passed over the frozen wastes between Iceland and the north of Norway. Needless to say, even by the time it reaches us, this air will still be very icy, cold and raw.

But another factor makes matters even worse. You will recall that not only does the wind flow along the isobars with low pressure to the left, its speed is also inversely proportional to the distance apart of the isobars themselves; the closer they are together, the stronger the wind. And if you watch successive weather charts for the next few days, either in your *Irish Times* or on the television, you will notice that as time passes, the isobars squeeze closer and closer together. In other words, it will not just be cold, it will be very windy too; and when low temperatures and strong winds come together, wind chill plays a significant part in how we feel.

Low temperatures in themselves are not particularly unpleasant when the air is still. We can feel relatively comfortable because we are encapsulated in an envelope of stationary air whose innermost layers adapt to the body temperature, insulating it effectively from the cold, surrounding atmosphere. But even the lightest breeze will disturb and blow away this protective, invisible cocoon, and then the cold wind quickly carries away whatever heat our bodies may produce. In general, for a given combination of clothing and air temperature, the higher the wind speed, the colder any individual will feel.

It is for this reason that a wind chill factor is sometimes included in the weather forecast. The wind chill equivalent temperature, to give it its full name, is not an actual temperature at all, but a conceptual assessment of the influence of the wind on the perceived temperature; it is a measure of discomfort, rather than a reading from any real or imaginary thermometer.

The notion is popular because we have all from time to time felt chilled by a stiff breeze when standing in the cold. But the figure should not be taken too literally; the extent to which we feel cold or otherwise involves many other factors, including how much clothing we have on, our age and physical condition, and whether we are physically active at the time or not.

Gale on the Seafront (oil on canvas), René François Xavier Prinet (1861–1946)
Private Collection/Giraudon/The Bridgeman Art Library

A Topical Tip: How to Build an Igloo

25 November 2005

Officially, this is still the autumn, but we have begun already to feel 'the icy fang and churlish chiding of the winter's wind'. But we are lucky; we have to brave such harsh conditions only now and then. For inhabitants of the far north, however, swirling snow and icy winds are a normal, everyday experience, and they face particular challenges in providing themselves with shelter from these hostile elements.

In the southern parts of their domain, the Inuit peoples can avail of stones and limited quantities of wood to make their huts, but from time to time in winter their hunting activities take them to places where the only available building material is snow. There their survival depends upon the igloo, a masterpiece of structural strength combined with thermally efficient engineering.

Firstly, the heat inside in igloo causes a vapour-proof glaze to form upon the snow-packed walls. Then the powerful insulating capabilities of snow ensure that those inside enjoy a temperature regime that is at least 10 degrees warmer than the air outside, and the living area is entirely draught-proof. Moreover, the igloo's hemispherical geometry presents the smallest possible external surface area for any given volume, so that loss of heat by radiation is as low as possible.

An igloo can be constructed fairly quickly, but it requires skill and experience to get it right. The snow, for example, must be exactly right in density; if it is too soft it crumbles, and if it is too hard, it will break up into sharp, misshapen, quite unmanageable slabs.

Having found the right snow, the igloo builder cuts it into slightly concave blocks, which are then set on edge to form a circle. The top surface of the base is shaved so that successive rows of blocks will form an ascending spiral, narrowing with height. The roof is capped with a keystone, a wedge-shaped block of ice carefully sculpted to be wider at the top than at its base, and then the gaps between the blocks over the whole surface of the igloo are grouted with additional quantities of snow.

At this point the structure is a fragile one, and could crumble easily if treated carelessly. Resilience is provided by lighting a whale-blubber lamp inside the igloo and then closing up the entrance with a block of ice. The snow on the inner surface starts to melt, but because of the igloo's vaulted shape the water does not drip, but rather soaks gradually into the blocks, wetting them for a considerable proportion of their depth. The final step is to unblock the entrance and remove the lamp, allowing a surge of cold air to transform the inside of the structure into a dome of solid ice, strong enough to allow a polar bear to crawl across the roof – which one sometimes does – without causing any damage.

Igloo, Michael Olson
photos.com

Divers Interpretations of a Triple Sun

28 November 2005

The Wars of the Roses are almost impossible to fathom. They hinge on the two younger sons of King Edward III: John of Gaunt, the Duke of Lancaster, and Edmund of Langley, Duke of York. The throne of England oscillated between rival descendants of these two Dukes for over 30 years in the latter half of the fifteenth century, with many a rousing battle in between. At one of these, the Battle of Mortimer's Cross in February 1461, Lancastrian forces faced their Yorkist counterparts under Edward, Earl of March, who not long afterwards was to take over as King Edward IV.

A contemporary chronicler describes what came about: 'The Monday before the day of battle, about 10 o'clock, were seen three suns in the firmament shining full clear, whereof the people had great marvel, and thereof were aghast. The noble Earl Edward them comforted and said, "be of good cheer and dread not; this is a good sign, for these three suns betoken the Father, the Son and Holy Ghost." '

Shakespeare in *Henry VI, Part 3*, however, puts a rather different slant on things. 'Dazzle mine eyes,' he has Edward suddenly exclaim, 'or do I see three suns?' His brother Richard confirms the apparition:

> *Three glorious suns, each one a perfect sun;*
> *Not separated with the racking clouds,*
> *But severed in a pale clear-shining sky.*

And Shakespeare plays on words to present the occurrence as auguring the advancement of Edward, Richard and their brother George, the three sons of the Duke of York, recently deceased. 'Tis wondrous strange,' Edward modestly continues:

> *I think it cites us, brother, to the field,*
> *That we, the sons of brave Plantagenet,*
> *Each one already blazing by our meeds,*

Should, notwithstanding, join our lights together,
And over-shine the earth, as this the world.

Nowadays, however, we recognise 'three suns' as an optical phenomenon variously called 'mock suns', 'sun dogs', or by meteorologists, *parhelia*. The two apparent images of the solar disc are located 22 degrees on either side of the real sun, each a segment of a solar halo.

A halo occurs when the sun is shielded by a thin cloud of ice crystals. Each crystal resembles a hexagonal cylinder in shape, like a short pencil but tiny by comparison. A ray of light striking one of the sides of a hexagonal prism is refracted, or 'bent', as it passes through the ice by an amount close to 22 degrees. So, given a more or less random orientation of the crystals, an observer will see the sun surrounded by a complete 22-degree halo.

But if the ice crystals are predominantly flat, as sometimes happens, they tend to settle horizontally, as falling leaves do. In such circumstances, an observer sees refracted light only from the two sides of where the solar halo ought to be, and the resulting two spots on either side of the sun resemble images of the sun itself.

Vädersolstavlan, **Jacob Elbfas** (1600–64), *after* **Urban Malare**, *1630s, Storkyrkan, Stockholm.* Wikipedia, Creative Commons

Capturing the Atmosphere on Canvas

5 December 2005

'Without the fog, London would not be a beautiful city.' Few today would be inclined to share this view of Monet, but it must be conceded that in his paintings of the Thames, it is the meteorology – the light-filled fog and mist – rather than any intricacies of the local architecture, that dominates virtually every scene.

Claude Oscar Monet was born in Paris in 1840, but spent his formative years in the port of Le Havre in Normandy. While still a student in the 1860s, he was introduced by the artist Eugène Boudin to the practice, then very uncommon, of painting *en plein air*, 'in the open air', and he went on to become the initiator, leader and unswerving advocate, almost indeed the personification, of the Impressionist movement in the late nineteenth and early twentieth centuries.

Even in his very early paintings, however, Monet was meteorologically precise. His *Regatta at Sainte-Adresse,* painted in 1867, portrays the beach at Le Havre looking east-southeast into the mouth of the river Seine. The water sparkles in the evening sun, and decaying cumulus clouds, formed earlier by the heating of the land on the far bank of the river, dot the sky in the distance. In the foreground of the picture a thin, broken layer of cirrostratus can be seen advancing from the west, clearly the first signs of an approaching warm front.

Monet's very next painting, *The Beach at Sainte-Adresse*, may well, the experts tell us, have been begun later that same afternoon, and in this we see the sky already covered by a thickening layer of altostratus; all the brightness has departed from the scene, and rain is clearly imminent.

The *Regatta* and the *Beach* represent the first signs of an engaging Monet trait: that of painting the same scene time and time again under different light and atmospheric conditions. He did the same, for example, with a series of views of haystacks in 1891, with Rouen Cathedral in 1894, with water lilies in his garden in his closing years, and of course, with the Houses of Parliament in London, most notably in 1904. Like his fellow Impressionists working out of doors, he was aware that everything we see must be viewed through, and is affected by, the atmosphere.

It was for this reason that he was fascinated by the London fogs. *Effet de Brouillard,* for example, shows the spires of the Parliament buildings silhouetted through a soupy atmosphere of smoky purples, blues and greys; and in *Houses of Parliament: Sun Breaking through the Fog,* the sun itself is reduced to a mere feeble ball of light. 'It is the air surrounding the bridge, the buildings and the boat I wish to paint,' he said. 'I want to capture the beauty of the atmosphere in which these objects are located.'

Claude Monet died at his home in Giverny in Normandy on this day, 5 December, in 1926.

The Beach at Sainte-Adresse, 1867 (oil on canvas), **Claude Monet** (1840–1926)
The Art Institute of Chicago, IL, USA /Giraudon/The Bridgeman Art Library

Wet Weekday Winners

13 December 2005

Meteorology has anarchists with an affinity for certain weekdays. Their methods are entirely peaceful, but they nonetheless cause irritation in the ranks of their more staid, conservative colleagues by suggesting, with evidence that is often plausible, that it rains more on certain days of the week than it does on any other. The orthodox view, naturally, is that all days in this respect are equal, and that none – in an Orwellian sense – should be more equal than the others.

Back in the 1920s, for example, a meteorologist from Lancashire called Ashworth spent many happy years examining climatological data for his native Rochdale. He found Sunday to be the driest day of the week, and also discovered that on weekdays there was more rain during working hours than there was in the evenings or at night, with the reverse the case on Sundays.

Then in the 1960s another man called Walters looked at London rainfall over a six-year period. He found that during the summer months, Tuesday was the wettest day, followed, in order, by Saturday, Thursday, Friday, Wednesday and Sunday; Monday was his driest day, with its average rainfall amounting only to three-quarters that of Tuesday.

George Nicholson, however, is very much a Thursday man. As an amateur meteorologist, he gathered rainfall data for more than 40 years at his home in Teddington, near London. He noticed back in 1963 that his readings showed Thursday to be the wettest day of the week, and claimed that the pattern persisted for the remainder of the century. According to his findings, a total of 143 inches of rain fell on Thursdays between 1953 and 2000, compared with only 125 inches on Sundays – the day which he found, like Ashworth, to be the driest of the seven.

Prima facie, such findings should be groundless. Although loosely based on a quarter of a lunar month, the seven-day week, from a scientific viewpoint, is an entirely arbitrary division of time introduced by humans purely for their own convenience, and to which Nature ought to be oblivious. Moreover, sceptical meteorologists will point out to you that if you separate the rainfall figures for any given period into seven lots corresponding to the weekdays, the totals will never coincide exactly; one of the seven days must inevitably turn out to be the wettest, and another to be the day on which the least amount of rain has fallen.

But, on the other hand, one can find possible explanations for anomalies. Human habits, after all, vary markedly from day to day, and in particular, many of our factories close their gates at weekends and commuters keep their motor-cars at home. This behaviour should result in less pollution and less waste heat being expelled into the atmosphere on Saturdays and Sundays than on working days, and it is not impossible that these factors may have a marginal effect on our weather.

*Very Unpleasant Weather, or the Old Saying verified "Raining Cats, Dogs and Pitchforks!",
published by G. Humphrey, 1820 (engraving),* **George Cruikshank (1792–1878)**
Private Collection/The Bridgeman Art Library

Emma's Dreary Summer

16 December 2005

The English novel is said to have begun with the writings of Daniel Defoe, Henry Fielding and others in the early eighteenth century. It is in the work of Jane Austen, however, that the novel assumed its distinctively modern character; she was the first to describe ordinary people coping as best they could with the unremarkable happenings of daily life, a refreshing change from the romantic melodrama theretofore in vogue. Austen was only 41 when she died in 1817; she was born 230 years ago today, on 16 December 1775, in the Hampshire village of Steventon where her father, George Austen, was the local clergyman.

Of Austen's six novels, *Emma* is the most meteorological by far. The action takes place over a 12-month period beginning in September of an unnamed year, and unfolds against a backdrop of dramatic weather. Throughout the book, emotions respond directly to this weather: when it is bright and sunny, everyone is cheerful; when it rains, misery abounds; and when it is hot and sultry, danger and romance are lurking in the heavy air.

By our experience, the weather portrayed in *Emma* seems strange and unfamiliar. The winter is plausible enough, 'the ground being covered with snow, and the atmosphere being in that unsettled state between frost and thaw, every morning beginning in rain or snow and every evening setting in to freeze'. But the climax of the novel occurs around midsummer, when the main protagonists are at Box Hill, near Donwell Abbey, and it is here that we encounter what for many years was gloated over as Jane Austen's famous 'error': 'rich pastures, spreading flocks, orchards in blossom, and light columns of ascending smoke'. 'Apple blossoms in late June?' the critics cried. 'Impossible!'

Meteorologists, however, have noted that the book was written between January 1814 and March the following year. Around that time, there had been several major volcanic eruptions around the world, most notably that of Mount Soufrière on St. Vincent's Island in the Caribbean in 1812; the pall of fine dust which these events infused into the atmosphere blocked radiation from the sun and caused the weather to be memorably harsh. The winter of 1813/14 was severe with very low temperatures and the following summer was unusually hesitant to appear, with May and June 1814

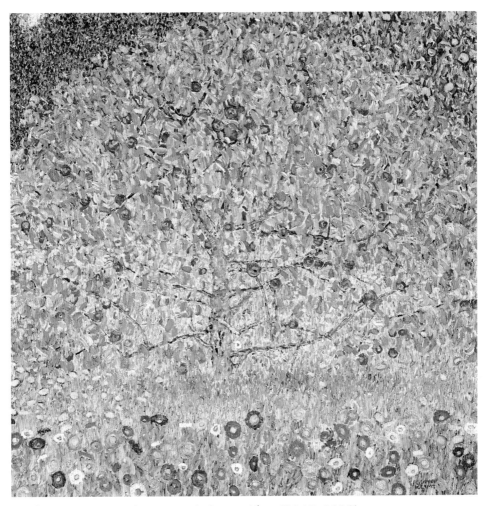

Apple Tree I, 1912 (oil on canvas), **Gustav Klimt (1862–1918)**
Private Collection/Photo © Christie's Images/The Bridgeman Art Library

being so chilly that many apple trees did not come into flower until well into what ought to have been summer.

Austen, indeed, describes a dismal start even to July. 'The evening was long and melancholy, and the weather added what it could of gloom. A cold, stormy rain set in and nothing of July appeared but in the trees and shrubs, which the wind was despoiling, and the length of the day, which only made such cruel sights the longer visible.' Only later in July 1814, both in *Emma* and in real life, did a normal summer finally appear.

Interplanetary Solutions to Excessive *Embonpoint*

17 December 2005

'Let me have men about me that are fat,' says Shakespeare's Julius Caesar, looking suspiciously across the Roman street at skinny Cassius. 'Sleek-headed men,' the mighty Julius wants, 'and such as sleep o' nights'. The pool of potential boon companions meeting the criterion laid down by Caesar is always very adequate, but it will be augmented in the coming weeks when many of us, having overindulged throughout the Christmas season, find ourselves temporarily challenged by our *embonpoint*.

We have each of us at any given time, and whether troubled by our *embonpoint* or not, a certain quality we think of as our 'weight'. It is a consequence of gravity, which is in turn a manifestation of the mutual attraction between us and the planet on which we find ourselves; it is denoted by a number which we often feel is higher than it ought to be, and which, from time to time, we try to change to a smaller one.

The figure we associate with our weight depends not only on our personal *avoirdupois*, but also on the gravitational characteristics of our planet. In theory we could reduce our weight by living on a different one, and in general, the smaller the planet, the lower would be the force of gravity upon its surface – although the density of the material making up the planet also plays a part. If life were virtual reality, a virtual voyage to a distant world could be used to reduce one's weight quite painlessly. So let's indulge ourselves inconsequentially and evoke

> *. . . that blessed mood,*
> . . . .
> *In which the heavy and the weary weight*
> *Of all this unintelligible world is lightened. . .*

The best weight-watcher locations in this galaxy are Mars and Mercury. Gravity on both these planets is a mere 40 per cent of that on Earth, so a beamed-up 12-stone Earthling might expect to feel as if he weighed only four and a half stone as he skipped nimbly across the rugged surfaces of these other worlds. But there are disadvantages to both; when we look at the weather prospects our athletic virtual traveller might expect, we find that Mercurian days are always boiling hot, and that the temperature on Mars is usually well below the freezing point.

Our 12-stone man, if transported hence to Uranus, would have his weight reduced to only ten stone seven, which he might conclude was hardly worth the bother. He would tip the scales at much the same amount on Venus, and on Saturn his weight would be almost identical to that on Earth. On Neptune, however, he would carry 17 stone, and on Jupiter a massive 31.

But by far the best weight-watcher's haven is nextdoor. If he could survive its lack of atmosphere, the average man on the Moon could hop around its surface like a two-year-old, since it would seem to him that he weighed just 27 pounds.

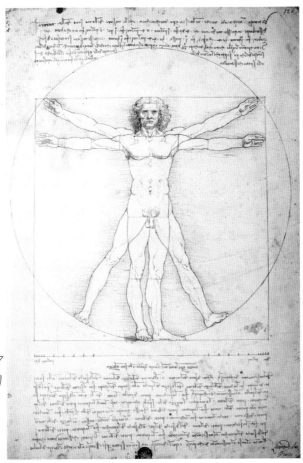

*Vitruvian Man, c.1487
(pen and ink on paper)*
Leonardo da Vinci
(1452–1519)
Simon Booth/
photos.com

A Canterbury Tidal Tale

19 December 2005

*T*he *Franklin's Tale,* one of the stories told by Chaucer's pilgrims on their way to Canterbury, is a tale of intrigue, magic and illicit love in mediaeval Brittany. It concerns a lady called Dorigen who was married to Arveragus, a noble knight, who was obliged to depart upon a voyage. While he is away, Dorigen develops a morbid fascination with a certain crop of rocks on the shore adjacent to the family castle, which she fears may wreck her husband's ship on his return:

> *But when she saw the grisly rocks all black,*
> *For very fear her heart would start aback. . .*

Now, a local lad, the young Aurelius, begins to fancy his chances with the Lady Dorigen, and to rid herself of his unwelcome attentions, Dorigen promises to consent to his advances whenever a certain event, which seems to her impossible, should happen; she will be his if ever those nasty rocks should disappear.

> *'I say, when you have made the coast so clean*
> *Of rocks that there is no stone to be seen,*
> *Then will I love you best of any man;*
> *Take here my promise – all that ever I can.'*

Nothing daunted, the wily Aurelius consults with a magician. The latter works his spells, and some months later, in 'the cold and frosty season of December', behold

> *. . . all the rocks by magic and his lore*
> *Appeared to vanish for a week or more.*

A year or two ago, it occurred to a clever and literary astronomer from Texas, Donald Olson, that there might be a grain of truth on Chaucer's tale. His theory was that the rocks might have disappeared because of abnormally high tides. He did some

Dorigen of Bretaigne, 1871 (watercolour), **Edward Burne-Jones (1833–98),** V&A Museum

calculations, and to his surprise he found that on this day, 19 December, in 1340, very near the time of Chaucer's birth, not only were the Sun, the Moon and Earth exactly in alignment, producing an eclipse, but the two former bodies were very nearly at their closest possible to Earth – a very rare combination that would clearly have produced exceptional tides.

Now Chaucer was himself an amateur astronomer, and is known to have visited France and might well have been aware of Brittany's dramatic tides. Could it be that as an adult, having checked his horoscope and discovered the unusual tide-raising potential of the astronomical configuration that occurred around the time he was born, Chaucer used it as the basis of *The Franklin's Tale*?

In any event, it all ends happily. Aurelius, ashamed, chivalrously releases Dorigen from her vow, and she confesses to Arveragus and is forgiven.

> *Which was most generous, do you think, and how?*
> *Pray tell me this before you farther wend.*
> *I can no more, my tale is at an end.*

Index

Picture Credits

1 harryfn, photos.com

3 Alexey Klementiev, photos.com

4 Ideeone, photos.com

7 Storm in Harvest, 1856 (oil on canvas), John Linnell (1792–1882) © The Drambuie Collection, Edinburgh, Scotland/The Bridgeman Art Library

13 Scene on Ice (detail), c.1620 (oil on wood panel), Hendrick Avercamp (1585–1634), National Gallery of Ireland

15 Snow Storm — Steam Boat off a Harbour's Mouth,1842 (oil on canvas), Joseph Mallord William Turner (1775–1851), Tate Collection

16 Darius Derics, photos.com

19 Mallard and Rime Frost, 1994 (oil on canvas), Julian Novorol (born 1949) Private Collection/The Bridgeman Art Library

21 The Winds Blowing Across the Lake at Lough Bray, Selina Crampton (1777–1858), Private Collection, London

23 The Gale on the Sea is Over, 1839 (oil on canvas), Ivan Aivazovsky (1817–1900), © The State Tretyakov Gallery, Moscow, Russia

25 Harmonia Macrocosmica, Amsterdam, 1660. Plate representing the planets' orbits according to the Tychonic system, Tycho Brahe (1546–1601). Milan, Biblioteca Ambrosiana. © 2012. © Veneranda Biblioteca Ambrosiana/De Agostini Picture Library/Scala, Florence

27 The French cavalry takes the Dutch fleet trapped in the ice at the port of Den Helder in the waters off Texel, 21 January 1795, Charles Mozin (1806–62) © RMN / Château de Versailles

29 Snow crystals, Wilson Bentley, Digital Archives of the Jericho Historical Society Wilson Bentley, snowflakebentley.com

31 Sleepy Old Woman,1656 (oil on canvas), Nicolaes Maes (1634–93), Royal Museums of Fine Arts of Belgium, Brussels

33 The Miracle of the Manna, c.1577 (oil on canvas), Jacopo Tintoretto (1518–94) Wikimedia Commons

34 Andreas Kaspar, photos.com

37 Printemps à Giverny, 1903 (oil on canvas), Claude Monet (1840–1926) Private Collection/ Giraudon /The Bridgeman Art Library

39 Hare,1502 (watercolour on paper), Albrecht Dürer (1471–1528), Graphische Sammlung Albertina, Vienna, Austria/ The Bridgeman Art Library

41 Country Road (oil on board),

Markey Robinson (1918–99), Private Collection/Photo © Bonhams, London, UK/Bridgeman Art Library

43 The Dream, 1912 (oil on canvas), Franz Marc (1880–1916), Madrid, Museo Thyssen-Bornemisza. © 2012. Museo Thyssen-Bornemisza/ Scala, Florence

45 Markree Castle, Co. Sligo, Alexey Zarodov © 2012 photos.com

47 Dirk Wiersma, Science Photo Library

49 Ms Fr 247 f.89 The Fall of Jericho, illustration from 'Antiquités Judaïques', c.1470 (vellum), Jean Fouquet (c.1420–80) and Studio Bibliothèque Nationale, Paris, France/ The Bridgeman Art Library

51 From The Little Mermaid, Harry Clarke (1889–1931), National Gallery of Ireland

53 L'Averse (The Downpour), 1893 (oil on canvas), Paul Serusier (1863–1927), Musée d'Orsay, Paris/RMN/Hervé Lewandowski

55 Portrait of William Wordsworth photos.com

57 Jonas Hanway Pioneers the First Umbrella in London,19th-century engraving

59 Dutch Windmills, 1884 (oil on canvas), Eugène Boudin (1824–98), Musée de la Chartreuse, Douai

61 St Benedict, 1441 (fresco), (c.1387–1455) Wikipedia Commons

63 The Fighting Temeraire, 1839 (oil on canvas), Joseph Mallord William Turner (1775–1851) National Gallery, London, UK/The Bridgeman Art Library

65 Earth and Moon, NASA

67 Walpurgisnacht (Night of the Witches),1946 (oil on canvas), Ary Stillman (1891–1967) Indianapolis Museum of Art, Gift of the Stillman-Lack Foundation

68 Jupiter Images, photos.com

71 Sunrise Mist, Ontario, Canada, Pavel Chaiko, photos.com

73 Portrait of William Rowan Hamilton, Autotype from photograph taken in 1857, Fulneck, Yorkshire/ Library of Congress

75 Thomas Malthus, 1833, John Linnell (1792–1882). By permission of the Master of Haileybury and ISC.

77 The Lock on the Stour (oil on canvas), after John Constable, at Angelsea Abbey © National Trust Images

79 The Violin, 1916 (oil on wood panel), Juan Gris (1887–1927), Kunstmuseum, Basle, Switzerland Giraudon/The Bridgeman Art Library

81 La Grenouillère, 1869 (oil

on canvas), Claude Monet (1840–1926) Metropolitan Museum of Art, New York, USA/The Bridgeman Art Library

83 Irish stamp

85 Nocturne — Red Tide (oil on canvas) Anne McWilliams

87 Priestess of Delphi, 1891 (oil on canvas), John Collier (1850–1934) Art Gallery of South Australia, Adelaide, Australia/Gift of the Rt. Honourable, the Earl of Kintore 1893/ The Bridgeman Art Library

89 The Great Wave off Kanagawa, c.1831 (woodblock print), Katsushika Hokusai (1760–1849) Wikimedia, Creative Commons

91 Noctilucent clouds © Daragh McDonough

93 Map of Ireland, Topographia Hiberniae, National Library, Dublin

95 Wellington at Waterloo, 1892 (oil on canvas), Ernest Crofts (1847–1911), Private Collection Photo © Bonhams, London, UK/The Bridgeman Art Library

97 Landscape at Dusk, 1885 (oil on canvas), Vincent Van Gogh (1853–90) Madrid, Museo Thyssen-Bornemisza © 2012 Museo Thyssen-Bornemisza Madrid

99 Midsummer Eve, c.1908 (watercolour on paper), Edward Robert Hughes (1851–1914) Private Collection/ Photo © The Maas Gallery, London/The Bridgeman Art Library

101 Old Man in Sorrow (On the Threshold of Eternity) 1890 (oil on canvas), Vincent Van Gogh (1853–90)/Rijksmuseum Kröller-Müller, Otterlo, The Netherlands/The Bridgeman Art Library

103 Statue of Zeus, after Phidias at the State Hermitage Museum. George Shuklin, Wikipedia Commons

104 Artur Bogacki, photos.com

107 The Three Sisters of Dean Liddell (oil on canvas), Sir William Blake Richmond (1842–1921); Private Collection. The Bridgeman Art Library

109 Whymper's Apparition (engraving) from Scrambles Across The Alps in 1860–69, Edward Whymper/TPI

111 Aurora Borealis, NASA

113 Diagram showing the process of magnetic reversal, NASA

115 The Starry Night,1889 (oil on canvas), Vincent Van Gogh (1853–90). The Museum of Modern Art, New York/The Bridgeman Art Library

117 The Great Fish Market, 1603 (oil on oak panel), Jan Brueghel (1568–1625) From the Mannheim

Gallery © bpk/Bayerische Staatsgemäldesammlungen

119 Harvest Home, Sunset 1856 (oil on canvas), John Linnell (1792–1882) © Tate Gallery

121 Indian satellite image showing monsoon clouds over the subcontinent. India Meteorological Department

123 A Deluge, c.1517–18 (pen & ink with wash on paper), Leonardo da Vinci (1452–1519) The Royal Collection © 2011 Her Majesty Queen Elizabeth II/The Bridgeman Art Library

125 Still Life with Bible, 1885 (oil on canvas), Vincent Van Gogh (1853–90). Van Gogh Museum, Amsterdam, The Netherlands/The Bridgeman Art Library

127 International Time Zones. Wikipedia, Creative Commons

129 Study of Cirrus Clouds, c.1822 (oil on paper), John Constable (1776–1837) Victoria & Albert Museum, London, UK/The Bridgeman Art Library

131 Cloud study, 1981-862/1, c.1803-1811 (pink and grey wash), Luke Howard (1772–1864), Light cirrocumulus beneath cirrus. Inscribed in pencil: Cirrus, Royal Meteorological Society

133 Man Catching Bees,14th century. British Library

135 Nova 2644 fol.94v Beehives, from 'Tacuinum Sanitatis' (vellum), Italian School (14th century) Osterreichische Nationalbibliothek. Vienna, Austria/Alinari /The Bridgeman Art Library

136 Comstock, photos.com

139 Set of eight Greek stamps showing the eight winds depicted on the Horologion of Andronicus.

141 The Persistence of Memory,1931 (oil on canvas), Salvador Dali (1904–89) Museum of Modern Art, New York, USA/The Bridgeman Art Library

143 Cupid Unfastening the Girdle of Venus,1788 (oil on canvas), Sir Joshua Reynolds (1723–92) Hermitage, St. Petersburg, Russia/The Bridgeman Art Library

145 Coming From Evening Church, 1830 (mixed media), Samuel Palmer (1805–81) © Tate Gallery

147 Side view of the Victory of Samothrace (Parian marble). Peter Willi, Louvre, Paris, France/The Bridgeman Art Library

149 Foucault's Pendulum, photos.com

151 The Source of the Arveyron, 1781 (pen and ink and watercolour on paper), Francis Towne

(1739–1816) © Tate Gallery

153 Terceira, engraved by Edward Finden, after a painting by Warren Henry (1794–1879), Private Collection/Bridgeman Art Library

154 Michael Fritzen, photos.com

157 Lisbon,1755, G.M. Burghry, Jan Kosak Collection

159 A Woman Baking Bread,1854 (oil on canvas), Jean-François Millet (1814–75) Collection Kröller-Müller Museum, Otterlo, The Netherlands

161 Page from Codex Leicester, showing a diagram of Earthshine, amongst other items, Leonardo da Vinci (1452–1519), Corbis

162 Canute holding back the waves, engraving. photos.com

165 (top) Johann Gottlob Leidenfrost (1715–94) Wikipedia Commons; (bottom) Photograph, Ilya Lisenker, University of Colorado, Boulder

167 Gale on the Seafront (oil on canvas), René François Xavier Prinet (1861–1946). Private Collection/ Giraudon/The Bridgeman Art Library

169 Igloo, Michael Olson. photos. com

171 Vädersolstavlan, Jacob Elbfas (1600–64), after Urban Malare, 1630s, Storkyrkan, Stockholm. Wikipedia, Creative Commons

173 The Beach at Sainte-Adresse,1867 (oil on canvas), Claude Monet (1840–1926). The Art Institute of Chicago, IL, USA / Giraudon/The Bridgeman Art Library

175 Very Unpleasant Weather, or the Old Saying verified "Raining Cats, Dogs and Pitchforks!", published by G. Humphrey, 1820 (engraving), George Cruikshank (1792–1878). Private Collection/The Bridgeman Art Library

177 Apple Tree I, 1912 (oil on canvas), Gustav Klimt (1862–1918). Private Collection/ Photo © Christie's Images/The Bridgeman Art Library

179 Vitruvian Man, c.1487 (pen and ink on paper) Leonardo da Vinci (1452–1519) Simon Booth/ photos.com

181 Dorigen of Bretaigne, 1871 (watercolour), Edward Burne-Jones (1833–98), Victoria & Albert Museum

All images are © copyright individual rights holders unless stated otherwise.

Every effort has been made to trace copyright holders not mentioned here. If there have been any omissions, the publishers will be happy to rectify this in a reprint.